Why the Chicken Crossed the Road

&

OTHER HIDDEN ENLIGHTENMENT
TEACHINGS FROM THE BUDDHA TO
BEBOP TO MOTHER GOOSE

Dean Sluyter

ILLUSTRATED BY MAGGY SLUYTER

Most Tarcher/Putnam books are available at special quantity discounts for bulk purchases for sales promotions, premiums, fund-raising, and educational needs. Special books or book excerpts also can be created to fit specific needs. For details, write or telephone Putnam Special Markets, 200 Madison Avenue, New York, NY 10016; (212) 951-8891.

Jeremy P. Tarcher/Putnam
a member of Penguin Putnam Inc.
200 Madison Avenue
New York, NY 10016

Library of Congress Cataloging-in-Publication Data
Sluyter, Dean.
Why the chicken crossed the road : and other hidden enlightenment teachings from the Buddha to bepop to Mother Goose / by Dean Sluyter.
p.   cm.
ISBN 0-87477-905-7 (alk. paper)
1. Spiritual life.   I. Title.
BL624.S593   1998
291.4'4—dc21   97-40980   CIP

Printed in the United States of America

1   3   5   7   9   10   8   6   4   2

This book is printed on acid-free paper. ∞

Book design by Judith Stagnitto Abbate

Why
the Chicken
Crossed the Road

Jeremy P. Tarcher/Putnam

A M E M B E R O F

Penguin Putnam Inc.

N E W Y O R K

Thank You

※

—to Apu, Stan Berman, Chuck Coe, Naradarishi Dasa, Antoine duBourg, Jack Dufford, John Hanly, Dr. Fred Kingsbury, Rabbi William Kraus, John Makransky, Matthew Mandelbaum, John McBride, John Platt, Mary Platt, Barbara Mae Stockhoff, P. J. Tyler, Barin Van Krugel, Speed Weed, Roy Wepner, and Andrew Zwick for their kind suggestions, assistance, information, and support; to Jane Cavolina for her indispensable guidance; to Ria Cooper, Susan Dineen, Gideon Lewis-Kraus, and Jim Vincent for their sensitive reading of the manuscript; to Gretchen and Bill Richardson for their warm hospitality; to The Pingry School for nurturing me; to my students for teaching me; to Phil Goldberg for many years of generous advice and writerly encouragement; to my stalwart agent, Jonathan Matson; to the Venerable Jeremy Tarcher, my editor and friend; to Joel Fotinos, Irene Prokop, Jocelyn Wright, and the rest of the impossibly patient, helpful crew at Tarcher; to John Frisius of Van Nuys High School, whose passion still inspires me every day; to A. C. Bhaktivedanta Swami, Rabbi Shlomo Carlebach, Maharishi Mahesh Yogi, Jerry Jarvis, Nadine Lewy, Rick Stickles, Sheikh Muzaffereddin Halveti al-Jerrahi, Ram Dass, Neem Karoli Baba, Kedar Harris, Suil, Ngak'chang Rinpoche, Khandro Déchen, Lama Surya Das, Khenpo Sonam Tobgyal Rinpoche, Lama Yeshé Gyamtso, Brendan Kennedy, Charles Genoud, and my other kind Teachers, past, present, and omnipresent; and to Maggy, Day, and Tara, who brought the hitchhiker in from the cold.

FOR MY PARENTS

Harris Sluyter
1921–1988

Amelia G. Sluyter
1923–1993

Contents

※

EXPLODING PROVERBS

ACCIDENTAL HYMNS

How wonderful! How wonderful!
All things are enlightened exactly as they are.

—THE BUDDHA
(upon attaining enlightenment)

✳

"Tut, tut, child," said the Duchess.
"Everything's got a moral if only you can find it."

—LEWIS CARROLL
Alice's Adventures in Wonderland

Introduction:
Radio free Buddha

$\mathcal{G}$OD SINGS in the shower. He croons, She warbles, It yodels, They chant. Some of us, as we pass by the window, catch an odd phrase accidentally and then walk on, humming, wondering where we heard it. Others stand vigil, dutifully taking notes, searching for logic and system in God's sublime improvisation. Comparing their findings later, they argue heatedly over what God sang— depending on when they listened, where they stood, what kind of pencil they used, and how sharp their ears are. Some of the most meticulous stenographers may be tone-deaf.

If we look closely at their transcriptions, though, and don't take too seriously any of their claims to have caught the One True Melody, we might find some subtle current running through it all, some hint of the warm pulse and ecstatic mind behind the measureless symphony they've tried to measure. And if we listen to the tunes hummed by the casual passersby, we might find that they capture even more faithfully the gigantic ease and spectacular range of the original Singer.

But that's just a metaphor. Here's another:

We're all sleeping buddhas—enlightened beings of perfect wisdom, equanimity, and compassion, who have yet to awaken to our own magnificence. We don't need to add anything to our state; we only need to realize it. Sooner or later the alarm goes off. The clock radio we set in some forgotten aeon blares the clear signal of Radio Free Buddha, blasting the shackles of ignorance from our minds, blowing away the morning cobwebs that obscure our innate Vastness.

What songs does Radio Free Buddha play? It hardly matters. The station's sage disc jockeys might spin the same pop tunes we hear on the radio today . . . or the cowboy songs we learned in the third grade . . . or the Tin Pan Alley ballads that brought our parents or grandparents together to make us. Between songs, they might entertain us with riddles and jokes, nursery rhymes and proverbs that were already clichés when we were children— stuff so subversively commonplace that we're guaranteed to repeat it indefinitely, unthinkingly. If we listen closely enough, *all* jokes are cosmic, *all* songs are hymns, *all* proverbs and nursery rhymes are booby-trapped with hidden enlightenment teachings. Even our homeliest cultural artifacts contain information that can incite our spiritual unfoldment.

Here's what I'm getting at: (1) Enlightenment—freedom, fulfillment, buddhahood, the kingdom of heaven, nonconceptual boundless Being—is our own nature, open to everyone, here and now, through direct experience, no belief required. (2) Because we intuitively know this good news already, we have planted covert hints of it throughout our culture, but then forgotten about them, like drunken pirates burying treasure and losing the map. (3) Excavating these hints is a fresh way of rediscovering the sacred in the mundane—of digging the cosmic ordinary.

In this book I have attempted some thirty-odd such excavations, and my little shovel has struck all sorts of surprises: "Knock-Knock, Who's There?" teaches the same process of radical self-inquiry advocated by Hindu masters; "Mary Had a Little Lamb" expounds the way of love and devotion as eloquently as the Gospels; "Home on the Range" celebrates the anarchic freedom of nirvana; "(I Can't Get No) Satisfaction" documents the frustrations of samsara; "Easy Does It," a principle as precise as $E=mc^2$, describes both the workings of the universe and the mechanics of meditation; "Why Did the Chicken Cross the Road?" summarizes the entire saga of the enlightenment journey.

Did the creators of these rhymes and lyrics consciously intend these implications? I assume not. But cosmic wisdom must lurk between the lines because it lurks everywhere. Everything (even in spite of itself) is multileveled, like a wedding cake, and I slice to the sacred level because that's where the sweet, creamy filling is.

In drawing out these hidden teachings, I have tried to show how comprehensive they are. They cover the basic questions confronting spring chickens first venturing across the spiritual road, as well as tricky problems that tough old birds may have been pecking at for some time. The most crucial issues keep reappearing, in different contexts and from different angles. It is said that the Buddha transmitted the Dharma (enlightenment

teaching) 84,000 different ways. Although enlightenment is unutterably simple, confusion is complicated, so for every variety
of confusion there's a different expression of Dharma to dispel it.

The songs and jokes hint at not only *why* we seek (why the
chicken crossed the road) and *what* to seek (the other side) but
how to seek, so I have included some practice suggestions relating to meditation and devotion, marriage and monasticism, giving, singing, dying, etc. You may want to try all or some or none
of these. Some are traditional, some strictly roll-your-own. I
think it's fine, especially in the early stages of exploration, to try
out an assortment of boots and binoculars. If a Buddhist meditation technique helps us enter the kingdom of heaven, Jesus
probably won't mind; if the parables of the New Testament help
us see nirvana, Buddha will no doubt rejoice. In the '60s, political radicals wore a button bearing Malcolm X's slogan: BY ANY
MEANS NECESSARY. That's still my attitude. We're Americans—
we eat pizza *and* sushi *and* blintzes, and if the mixture gives us an
occasional bout of heartburn, we can handle it.

Over the last thirty years I've meditated and chanted with yogis and lamas, *daven*ed with rabbis, danced with Sufi masters,
been hurled through the air by Aikido masters; I've spent
months at a stretch on retreats; I've studied scriptures and sutras.
But I'm not an expert on anything. I teach meditation, and an
unusual high-school course called Literature of Enlightenment
that's heavy on meditative lab work. But I'm not a Teacher. I am,
let's say, an entertainer who helps draw the crowd into the tent
before the Teacher comes onstage: a Gospel clown, a Dharma
juggler, who has had the lucky chance to meet some real Teachers, pester them with questions, and be inspired by them to

practice diligently. Hopefully this book will prompt you to learn (or keep learning) directly from such experts yourself.

Their teachings work. Boundless awareness, the ultimate clarity that resolves all questions and heals all wounds, really exists, really does transform our lives radically. If words like "enlightenment" seem too high-flown, perhaps it's enough to say that we really can be happy and genuine and kind; we really can be sane. Christ, Buddha, Socrates, Padmasambhava, Mirabai, Hallaj, Lao-tzu, Shankara, Dogen, the Baal Shem Tov were not merely abstract theorists or hopeful poets. They were navigators of the ocean of Being, whose pioneering routes can be followed by anyone who will read their maps and set sail. You don't have to wear a robe, and you don't have to go to India; liberative spiritual experience is open to anyone willing to adopt some simple practices and apply them persistently.

I SUSPECT THAT most of us, as young children, had a sense of some undefined special destiny—an intuition of surpassing inner greatness. Perhaps we fantasized that we were secretly Superboy, or the Lost Princess, or the future President. Then a year or two of lining up in school convinced us we were not so extraordinary after all. But we were right the first time. The surpassing greatness we vaguely sensed is our primordial nature, which is innate enlightenment; our special destiny is to fully realize that.

I hope this book will, in its peculiar way, help spark this realization by opening our ears to the transcendental message that assails us from all sides. If it works, you'll never again hear "Hey,

Hey We're the Monkees" or "I'm a Little Teapot" without hearing it as a wake-up call to the sleeping buddha that you are. Even better, you'll start hearing that wake-up call in *every* song and slogan—and, for that matter, in every car horn, thunderclap, chirping of crickets, and silence when the crickets stop.

The idea is not that far-fetched. The eighth-century Chinese Zen master P'an-shan had his first satori (enlightenment-glimpse) while walking through a marketplace. He overheard a customer tell the butcher, "Cut me some of the good stuff"; the butcher replied, "Hey, take a look—nothing but good stuff!" This was just the catalyst P'an-shan needed. He took a look, perhaps, at the ground, the sky, the people in their bustle of buying and selling . . . and everywhere he saw nothing but good stuff. In 1578 St. John of the Cross, while crouching in the dark, cramped dungeon where he had been imprisoned for months, heard a voice from the street singing a popular song:

> "Muérome de amores,
> carillo, ¿qué haré?"
> "¡Que te mueras—alahé!"

> *"I am dying of love,*
> *darling, what should I do?"*
> *"Just die then—what the hell!"*

Suddenly something inside him gave way: right there in his airless cell, clad in his lice-infested rags, he found himself letting go and "dying" into ecstatic union with the Infinite. Three centuries later, lucky Buddhist practitioners in the wilds of eastern

Tibet were jolted into enlightenment by the rugged huntsman-yogi Do Khyentse Rinpoche, who roamed about, waking people from their spiritual slumber with the blast of his muzzle-loading musket. My own first experience of transcendental awakening, in the family station wagon at the age of twelve, was triggered (I swear) by *Mad* magazine's "What—Me Worry?"

From the bottom of our morning cereal bowl, from the tail-lights of the car ahead of us, from the eyes of the stranger and our own eyes in the mirror—from every inch and moment of experience, the Subtle Vast One plays peekaboo with us. The Koran says, "Wherever you turn, there is the face of God." The Prajña-paramita Sutra says, "Every single mundane structure is the astonishing lion's roar of Perfect Enlightenment-Wisdom." That must include all the things we dismiss as trivial or irksome, from the gum on the sole of our shoe to the barking of the neighbor's dog. *Pay attention! Pay attention!*

WHAT HAPPENED to the chicken that stayed up all night to see where the sun came from? It finally dawned on him. May it finally dawn on us. May our eyes and ears be opened, and may we all get to the other side.

Cosmic Jokes

✳

1. What—me worry?

*T*RUE STORY: A San Fernando Valley afternoon in 1961. I'm twelve years old. My family is planning to see a drive-in movie later in the evening, and my mother sends me to the garage to clean out our Rambler station wagon. As I gather up the toys and clothes and comic books my brothers and I have left there, my hyperactive mind is, as usual, rehearsing and rehashing conversations, fretting over eventualities, calculating consequences. I am, as usual, utterly unaware of the noisy, agitated way my mind is functioning, both because my mind has *always* been this busy (I have nothing to compare it to) and because it *is* so busy (it's too caught up in chasing and snapping at its own tail to notice that it's caught up).

The next item I find on the backseat is a *Mad* magazine. I glance at the cover, with its picture of the magazine's idiot mascot, Alfred E. Neuman, and read his motto: **"What—Me Worry?"**

Time stops.

Suddenly it's as if my skull has been cracked open and emptied out. In an instant, my mind stops sizzling in its habitual static. In the vibrant silence that follows, I realize that this sizzle is what's called "worry," and that, until this moment, I've been doing it for as long as I can remember. My mind—freed at last from whipping itself through all those tortuous channels of how-come's and what-if's—becomes blissful clarity, perfect peace. I feel like an endless sky from which ancient, toxic clouds have been suddenly blown away. I am, in fact, floating in a bona fide state of satori, and I continue to float through the rest of the afternoon, the evening, the movie (*Parrish,* a plantation soap opera starring Troy Donohue), till bedtime, when I float blissfully into sleep.

The Sanskrit term for this phenomenon is *mahavakya*—"great utterance." When a master realizes that a disciple's mind has reached a moment of particular ripeness, he or she utters one of the classic formulations of cosmic Reality, perhaps a line from the Upanishads such as "Thou art That." And whammo: the disciple clearly, experientially Gets It. In my case the master was Sri Guru-ji Alfred E. Neuman. Well, the Lord moves in mysterious ways.

Or maybe not so mysterious. Maybe the Infinite reveals itself in ways that are exquisitely tuned to time, place, and audience. The most nagging worry of adolescents (*Mad's* traditional readership) is physical appearance. Is my chest too small? Is my nose too big? Braces? Acne? Alfred E. Neuman has splotchy freckles, protruding ears, ridiculous cheekbones, impossible hair, gap teeth, cockeyes . . . *and he doesn't worry!* Cheerfully oblivious to his funny looks, he embodies the teenager's chronic worry and explodes it away in the tension-release of laughter.

We Cold War kids also had some special, acute worries, which Alfred showed up just in time to ease. We grew up doing "drop drills"—huddling in silence under our desks with our hands clasped over the backs of our heads, waiting to see whether the next moment would bring nuclear Armageddon or the teacher's all-clear. And precisely in that moment of breathless, fearful anticipation lies the problem. Two thousand years earlier, Jesus diagnosed the condition and prescribed the cure:

Take therefore no thought for the morrow: for the morrow shall take thought for the things of itself.

The futility of worry is rooted in the element of time: worry is the agitated anticipation of what the world may do to us in the near or distant future. (Resentment is the agitated recollection of what the world did to us in the past. Guilt is the agitated recollection of what we did to the world—and often a convenient form of self-flagellation that allows us to keep doing it.)

The cure for worry, then (and resentment and guilt), is to live right now. This is not just some happy-face spiritual slogan, but the starkest realism—in fact it's our only option. We worry about tomorrow, but we always wake up today. It's never tomorrow, never five minutes from now, never one second from now. (When the future arrives, please raise your hand.) There's no time but the present, and even that is suspect.

In meditation you can see through the illusion of past, present, and future—your experience becomes the continuity of Nowness.

The past is only an unreliable memory held in the present. The future is only a projection of your present conceptions. The present itself vanishes as soon as you try to grasp it. So why bother with attempting to establish the illusion of solid ground?
                              —H.H. DILGO KHYENTSE RINPOCHE

Relinquishing the illusion of solid ground may seem scary at first; it does mean going into a kind of endless free-fall. But we're falling in delicious, total freedom indeed, with the growing realization that just as there is no ground to support us, there is no ground ever to hit.

Does living in liberated Nowness mean we can't work on Monday to get a paycheck on Friday? Or that we're not responsible for what we did in June because it's October? No—that would be flakiness, not enlightenment. We earn the right to be blasé about the illusory past and future only by being conscientious in the perpetual present. To the extent that we're functioning in a time-bound apparent world, we have to deal sensibly today with the seeds of probable tomorrows. But we don't have to be lost in agitation over the ways they may sprout.

This distinction became clear to me some twenty years after my *Mad* experience, in another automotive epiphany. A friend was driving me through some aggressively congested New Jersey traffic. He was holding forth passionately on some topic or other, making lots of emphatic gestures, looking to me for nods of agreement, and failing to note much of the sudden braking and lane-changing going on around him. Soon I felt my right foot stomping on the brake—the imaginary passenger-side brake that I had used for years in similar situations. Then suddenly, in mid-stomp, I realized: *This brake doesn't work*. It doesn't stop the car; it doesn't slow it down even a little. If the situation is truly dangerous, I should ask the driver to let me out (or better, to let me drive). Otherwise, I may as well relax and enjoy the ride.

I decided to renounce that imaginary brake. But suppressing the urge to stomp on it caused a whole new set of unpleasant sensations. My breathing grew constricted as I struggled to stifle my anxiety, and the tension I had denied to my right leg crept up into my gut. (Years later I became friends with some cops involved in dangerous assignments and discovered that they all had serious gastrointestinal problems.) Suppression, I realized, merely drives worry deeper into the psyche and the body, there to grow more toxic, resurfacing later in some other guise. So then I *truly* let go, of both worry and suppression. I breathed freely, my muscles relaxed, my tension evaporated.

We also have an *internal* passenger-side brake, which we stomp on incessantly. Worry about work, worry about family, worry about health . . . all involve futile straining for that brake and tensing ourselves against imagined crashes up the road. Whenever there is a practical way to grab the steering wheel of our destiny (work smarter, talk through the family problem, eat our healthy vegetables), we should certainly do so, but beyond that we may as well just breathe out and let go. Having done what we can, we can relax into the spacious freedom of simply Being and let whatever happens happen—which it will do whether we "let" it or not.

> *You have claim to your actions only; to their fruits you have no claim.*
>
> —BHAGAVAD GITA

This realization—that once we've done our best the chips are *going* to fall where they may—is profoundly liberating. But only if we want to be liberated. One stormy evening as I was leaving the school where I teach, I saw a mother standing under the front portico, peering anxiously up the driveway through the lightning and rain. She was, she explained, waiting for the bus to bring her son back from a fencing meet. When I suggested that she could relax in the faculty lounge with a cup of coffee, she smiled tightly: "No, I'll stay out here—I'm a worrier." Although worrying couldn't get the bus there a minute earlier, her job description as a good mother apparently required it. To stop would be to let go of that strained, unproductive self-definition, probably lifting considerable pressure off her children as well as herself.

If you had done everything in the past exactly the same except for the worrying, what would be different? What will you ever do in the future that worrying will improve?

while you worry about what each note means,
the band plays on.

you are running from a dog
who only chases because you run.
turn and face him.

though you hear the buzzing of the bee grow louder
be still.
do not fear a sting you have never felt,
you just might be a flower.

do not worry
about things falling into place.
where they fall
is the place
— MARK HARTLEY

SUGGESTIONS FOR FURTHER PRACTICE:

• Quit worrying (wouldn't you quit any other job that paid so poorly?), or at least take vacations. Breathe out and take your foot off that internal passenger-side brake for a day, an hour, even a moment. As you gain confidence that your universe does not crumble without the tension of worry to hold it together, extend your vacations.

• If that seems too hard, start by *watching* yourself worrying: "Ah, yes, this is called worry, it's something I choose to do." If even that's too hard, observe the worry of others. Note how much of their energy it consumes, and how it distorts the patterns of mind, speech, and body.

• Meditate. (More on this later.) The taste of transcendental ease that you catch through meditative practice will feed your faith that somehow everything's fundamentally okay. When you wake in the middle of the night gripped by anxiety, even the faint, lingering flavor of that transcendence can keep you from being overwhelmed.

• A yet more profound liberation into Nowness comes from abandoning hope as well as worry. But that's an advanced technique.

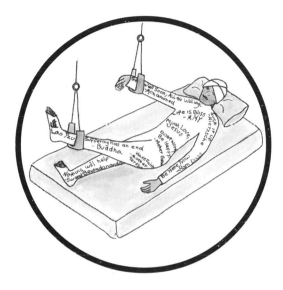

2. *Doctuh, it hoits*

PATIENT (gesturing awkwardly with his elbow):
"Doctuh, it hoits when I do like dis."
DOCTOR (imitating his gesture): "Don' do like dot!"

※

*J*N YOUR MIND'S ear, please hear the above exchange spoken with a thick Yiddish inflection. In your mind's eye, please see it performed by a couple of baggy-pantsed old comedians onstage at Grossinger's, the Granite, the Concord, any of the Catskills resorts where my grandparents sought relief from pre-air-conditioning New York City summers. This joke is the Borscht Belt Sutra, the concise summary of life's essential truth as contemplated by Jewish comedy, with its excruciatingly intimate knowledge of the nuances of suffering.

The Jewish culture of my grandparents elevated doctors to the status of M-Deities, and in this case the doctor has indeed displayed divine wisdom—effecting a total cure without recourse to surgery or drugs. Recognizing the Buddha's First and Second Noble Truths in the patient's complaint, the doctor responds with a deft application of the Third Noble Truth and a hint of the Fourth, thus opening the patient's eyes to his own overlooked wisdom and healing him instantaneously.

Dukkha, samudaya, nirodha, marga: suffering, origin of suffering, extinction of suffering, path to the extinction of suffering. In these Four Noble Truths, the topic of his first discourse after attaining enlightenment, the Buddha summarized the human predicament and what one can do about it. The doctor might call them symptom, diagnosis, prognosis, and treatment plan.

Doctuh, it hoits: *Dukkha* is pain, suffering, woe, misery. The Yiddish equivalent is the eloquent *tsooris* or *vey*, as in *Oy vey iz mir*, "O woe is me"—the Jewish mantra. And dukkha, said the Buddha, is universal. As the powerful R.E.M. song puts it, "Everybody hurts." (Hence substance abuse is such a stubborn habit. Everyone knows about its ravaging cumulative effects, but our need for anesthesia can be so urgent that we'll accept the damage if we can just go on numbing ourselves, one day at a time.) Shit happens to everybody, no matter how healthy or lucky or rich. At least the universality of the shitstorm may teach us to skip self-pity in favor of compassion. Your receding hairline is not a personal affront; your spouse's death is not an unprecedented tragedy.

Some kinds of suffering (earthquake, divorce, heart attack) are obvious and dramatic. Others are more subtle; dukkha covers everything from blinding agony to the vaguest unease. We sit upon the perfect hilltop watching the perfect sunset, but it's getting chilly and our bottom is growing sore. Our mammogram or HIV test comes back negative, but somewhere in the background of our joy the clock is already ticking toward the next test. As our stock soars we know that someone else's is diving, and we either suffer in quiet empathy or suffer the quiet hardening of heart that prevents empathy.

This subtle suffering is often repressed, the symptoms disregarded. Dukkha may be the First Truth because recognizing it is the first prerequisite for spiritual growth: if we don't admit that **it hoits**, we won't go see the **Doctuh** (the healer, teacher, guru, lama). We have learned to ignore our pain, as with a tight shoe we've been wearing for as long as we can remember. We spit-shine that shoe, we dress it up with fancy laces to distract ourselves from the pinch. But when we finally take it off, we're going to say *Ahhh!*

When I do like dis: The Second Noble Truth is *samudaya,* the origin of suffering. Sickness can be the most absorbing of hobbies, and a shiny new diagnosis, fresh from the doctor's office, is a prized conversation piece. But the patient has already made his own unwitting, surprising diagnosis. The cause of his painful symptoms is not an outer trauma or invading bug. He would *like* it to be some such alien agent, some nice, clearly defined Other with which to grapple. But his own complaint (as the doctor, that big party pooper, is about to show him) proves that *he's* making it hurt.

> *We have met the enemy and he is us.*
> —POGO

The human condition is not *inherently* painful; we experience it as painful only if we carry ourselves **like dis.** Dukkha arises not from what happens to us, but from how we process it. As a child you might have suffered to the point of tears because someone made a face at you or called you a poo-poo head; now the same name or face makes you laugh. It's hard to believe that your present pain, as viewed from the yet deeper level of maturity called enlightenment, is equally insubstantial, equally self-induced. But if you ascribe your pain to anything external (your job, your parents, your mate, your weight, your fate, your blah blah blah), then you're always at its mercy. If you see that you're the one who's making it hurt, then you're the one who can make it stop.

Which brings us to the Third Noble Truth: **Don' do like dot!** Since samudaya, the source of suffering, is internal, *nirodha,* the extinction of suffering, must be internal as well. This prognosis is good news indeed. Buddhist psychology makes a particular specialty of illuminating the subtle habits through which we create and maintain our pain. Once we've recognized these habits, we can start letting them go. The following experiment may provide a taste of this process.

1. Look at any object. I'm in the kitchen, so I'll use an apple. It's red, roughly spherical, and maybe three or four inches across. And although the apple appears to be "out there," on the table, our experience of it takes place within what we call "awareness" (wherever that is, and whatever it is). Now, when we see the apple, does our awareness itself become spherical, or red, or four inches across?

2. To clarify the issue, let's notice a second object—now I'm looking at a banana. Again, we become aware of the banana's attributes, but does our awareness itself become yellow or oblong? Clearly not, since we can experience both fruits at

once. To contain both shapes (and both colors and both sizes) at the same time, along with any number of possible additional objects, awareness itself must always be formless, colorless, sizeless.

3. Now, notice whatever sounds are present within awareness—refrigerator humming in the corner, catbird singing in the yard, truck rumbling down the street. Just as the ability of awareness to reflect varied forms points to its essential formlessness, doesn't its ability to reflect varied sounds point to its essential silence? Also notice that sensory information is spread out over space (seven inches of banana) and time (five seconds of birdsong). Doesn't the ability of awareness to reflect both time and space at once indicate that it is situated in neither time nor space—that it somehow rests outside of both?

4. Next, imagine that we experience some new, unprecedented object. No matter what that object might be, wouldn't it be reflected within this same silent, formless, timeless, spaceless openness we call awareness? And doesn't this point to an infinity of potential reflectivity?

Awareness, then (to use a favorite example of Buddhist teachers), is like a mirror, which changes its appearance but not its nature. It reflects whatever sizes, shapes, and colors are presented to it, yet maintains its own crystalline colorlessness, ineffable shapelessness, unbounded sizelessness. (If awareness is not unbounded, where are its edges? Any edges we can perceive or imagine are perceived or imagined *within* awareness.) It reflects all sounds, yet maintains its silence. Taste and smell work the same way. Even experiences of touch are reflections in mirrorlike, crystalline awareness; in that sense even touch doesn't touch us. But if the mirror gets confused and somehow clings to those reflections, identifies itself with them, then it becomes overwhelmed by the procession of colors and forms and forgets its own essential colorlessness. The experience of perfect, changeless boundlessness is lost in the field of change and boundaries—the field where suffering takes place.

5. Experiment further: Think some thought or recall some scene that you associate with happiness, comfort, or love. Now recall a scene associated with sadness or stress. Notice that both thoughts, along with the feelings they evoke, are reflected within mirrorlike, boundless awareness, which is as naturally free of thought and feeling as it is of sound and shape. Yet we so habitually cling to, identify with, lose ourselves in thoughts and feelings that we spend our lives pursuing the "happy" ones (and situations calculated to elicit them) and dodging the "sad" ones.

This process of identification is what makes us feel that *we're* shiny and new when we buy a shiny new car, and dented or rusted when (sooner or later) the car is. Identification is such an ingrained habit that it seems like a normal feature of life, but to the doctor's enlightened vision it's as clumsy and needlessly pain-inducing as the patient's odd gesture with his elbow.

No one can guarantee that we'll never have another toothache or fender bender. Of course we do what we can to avoid them. But it's by giving up our false identification with these experiences, by noticing that we are and always have been nothing but the crystalline awareness mirror within which these reflections frictionlessly come and go, that we accomplish the true extinction of suffering. It don't mean a thing if we ain't got that cling.

Coming, going, the waterbirds
Don't leave a trace,
Don't follow a path.
                            —DOGEN

Dukkha, samudaya, nirodha: Everybody hurts, everybody hurts themselves, everybody can stop hurting. Suffering happens, it happens due to the mistake of identification, but (hallelujah!) the mistake is correctable. Still, there's one Noble Truth not exhaustively covered by our doctor joke: *marga,* the path to the extinction of suffering. After a lifetime (or more) of clinging, *how* do we break that habit? How do we permanently open to our silent boundlessness, our natural freedom from the tides of suffering and change? In rare cases, one simple "Don' do like dot!" may shock us into a permanent cure. But if it doesn't, the doctor can prescribe some highly effective treatments that have been recommended for centuries by the most eminent specialists. That's what the rest of this book is about.

3. Knock-knock, who's there?

Knock-knock.
Who's there?
Arthur.
Arthur who?
Arthur any questions?

Knock-knock.
Who's there?
Frieda.
Frieda who?
Frieda prisoners.

(Etc.)

＊

*J*HIS IS THE riddle that first taught us about the emptiness of the notion of self. Again and again it poses philosophy's most fundamental question: Who are we? **Who's there?** Again and again, selves, names, personae (**Arthur, Frieda**) are tendered as answers. Again and again, we're lulled into accepting one of these named selves as valid. Then, the moment we look into it more closely (**Arthur who?**) it blows up in our face—the alleged self is annihilated, vaporized in a pun-fueled explosion of absurdity.

The setup for this joke, the gulling of the straight man, starts years earlier, in the crib, when deep, authoritative voices say, "Hello, Arthur. Cootchie-coo, Arthur. Is your diaper wet, Arthur?" Eventually they convince us we're this "Arthur" thing they keep talking about. As we grow, our idea of who or what is Arthur becomes more complex, a structure jerry-built out of bits of body image, personal history, and shifting psychological patterns. At some point we become interested in self-knowledge and assume that "knowing thyself" means sorting laboriously through all the layers of that complex structure till we find some kind of genuine, irreducible core—"the real me."

The masters say phooey to all that. Don't sort through—*cut* through. Beneath that wobbly Tinker-Toy-on-Jell-O edifice, dig the ground of pure Being.

> *As the habitual energy of projecting, crystallizing, grasping, routinizing and manipulating is released, consciousness can cease its constant and feverish fabrications of this allegedly substantial and independent me and mine.*
>
> —PRAJÑAPARAMITA SUTRA

To be sure, the cards seem stacked against us in this endeavor. All our interactions in time and space seem to require and corroborate the solidity of self. When we enter school, as if to avoid having our identity wash away in the sea of faces into which we're cast, we start using our surname; it adds the weight of reinforcements, the safety of numbers, to our personal identity. Now I'm not just Frieda, but Frieda Smith, and that Smith-ness resonates in the names and features of all my relatives. Thus Jesus exhorts us to transcend our earthbound sense of identity by transcending family identity:

> *Call no man your father upon the earth: for one is your Father, which is in heaven.*

And his words are echoed by a *koan* (an unanswerable Zen riddle designed to flip us out of illusory selfhood):

Show me the face you had before your father and mother met.

To bolster our sense of being real, and preferably permanent, we like to see our initials emblazoned on our shirts and license plates; our name on plaques, newspapers, or the spines of books. When we feel dislocated from our secure sense of identity—say, traveling alone in a strange city—we're eager to resolidify ourselves by reciting our name and story to the first person we meet. Even the way we write our names reinforces the exalted self: objects like a peach or chair or rock seem pretty real, but "Frieda," with its imposing capital letter, makes us *really* real. In English, we go so far as to capitalize "I," enshrining even the abstract notion of selfhood, independent of any Arthur or Frieda to pin it on.

But is a person such a distinct, definite, permanent, irreducible thing as that capital letter implies? What about those ordinary, non-person things? The peach, depending on when we look at it, might be a budding appendage of a peach tree or an amorphous mass of sugars quietly breaking down in our digestive tract. If we start using the legs of the chair for firewood, at precisely what point does the chairness vanish, and where does it go? Let's take the rock—*that* seems solid. It's *this* rock, Rock A, no question about its identity. But if we smash it with a hammer, which half is Rock A, and which is Rock B? Or are they both A? Or if they're B and C, where has A gone?

Now let's consider Amy the Amoeba. One day Amy undergoes asexual reproduction and splits in two. Where's Amy now? Is she both? Neither? If neither, who are these newcomers?

If there's now no definite Amy essence, did her splitting anni-
hilate it, or merely reveal that it never existed to begin with?
Since what we called "Amy" was itself the result of an earlier
splitting (and millions of splittings before that), was she ever
really Amy?

If a rock or an amoeba doesn't have a solid, unambiguous
identity, a "self," how can we be so sure a person does? Maybe
we have a "soul." But what *is* that—something we experience,
or just a rumor? Perhaps we've heard other rumors, drifting in
from the East, that rather than soul we are *Shunyata:* emptiness,
void. That may sound frightening, like some sort of black hole
of nothingness, some final drain down which everything swirls.
But even the concept of a hole or drain is just another concept.
Shunyata means that all our self-concepts are empty of reality,
including our concepts of emptiness.

We all probably have some intuition of this lack of a defin-
able self. Many of our neuroses may be uneasy responses to it,
such as the feeling of being inauthentic, an impostor among the
grown-ups, unequal to our responsibilities—and never suspect-
ing that the others feel like impostors too. Compulsive drinking
or overeating is probably an attempt to fill up the emptiness we
suspect is at our core. Compulsive sexual activity could be another way to reassure ourselves that we're solid and real: to experience something as intense as this orgasm, I must at least
exist; I hump, therefore I am. But we can't hump every moment, and then what will validate us? Possessions? (I own, therefore I am.) Power? (I control, therefore I am.) Knowledge? (I
know, therefore I am.) Obsession with celebrities? *They* must
exist, since everyone talks about them—to shine so brilliantly in
everyone's vision, these stars must have some special, extravivid

kind of reality. So, like thirsty vampires, we suck their presence any way we can.

> ESTRAGON: *We always find something, eh Didi, to give us the impression we exist?*
> VLADIMIR: *(impatiently) Yes yes, we're magicians.*
> —SAMUEL BECKETT, *Waiting for Godot*

There's nothing wrong with sex, food, knowledge, and the rest. But expecting them to give us solid selves is like trying to fill a sieve with water. An old proverb says, "You can drink too much, but you can never drink enough."

All this care and feeding of something that's not even there is so much work that eventually we're tempted to quit. Propping up the self, like hitting your head with a hammer, feels great when you stop. Suddenly you don't have to be smart, you don't have to be cool, you don't have to be good-looking—you don't have to be *nothin'* when you don't *be*. And when there's no self it's mighty difficult to be selfish or self-centered or self-righteous, not to mention self-conscious or self-effacing. Self-esteem is not even an issue.

Incidentally, nihilism and its city cousin, existentialism, both get this confrontation with emptiness half right. They see that the world offers no things of durable, absolute value, and that there is no durable, absolute self to enjoy such things anyway. Stripped of all traditional verities (God, meaning, self), we are left naked, absurdly buffeted by the ravages of time and chance, with no sure destination but the grave. But if the objects and values of the world are essentially empty, so are its ravages; and if there is no real self that accomplishes and enjoys, neither is there one that suffers. Existentialists perversely wallow in the bad news (nobody gets nothing) and ignore the good (nothing happens to nobody).

You are really the natural form of emptiness, so there is no need to fear. The Lords of Death too arise out of your own radiant mind, they have no solid substance. Emptiness cannot be harmed by emptiness.

—THE TIBETAN BOOK OF THE DEAD

So—how to do it? How to see through the notion of self, to cut through to liberating emptiness?

There are many ways. One is so simple we learned it at age four or five, the first time we played **Knock-knock.** Jesus points out this method's childish ease: "Ask, and it shall be given you; seek and ye shall find; knock, and it shall be opened unto you." All we have to do is keep knocking, keep on (insistently, penetratingly) asking the question **Who's there?** The great twentieth-century Indian saint Sri Ramana Maharshi recommended this method of self-inquiry as a universal technique for realization. Just keep asking, "Who's there?" or, in Ramana's version, "Who am I?" I'm driving to work. Fine—*who's* driving? I'm walking the dog—*who's* walking? Who is eating? Who is sleeping? Who's happy or depressed? Who experiences being "in" this body? Who is breathing, thinking, asking these questions? If these questions seem pointless and annoying, to whom do they seem so? Who's drunk? Who's bored? Who's furious? (Whoever or whatever it is, it's different from the fury itself. In becoming free from self, we become free from everything else.) Who experiences my experience? Can't find an answer to that one? *Who* can't?

We're not seeking any conceptual answer to this "Who am I?" The question becomes a kind of hammer for cracking open all limited concepts of self. (Who's conceptualizing?) It doesn't replace them with another concept: it reveals, directly and experientially, the underlying nonconceptual mystery. Like the punch line of our knock-knock joke, it blows away the false, limiting Arthur or Frieda. ("Blown away" is the literal meaning of *nirvana*.) This leaves us with . . . what? The Buddhist word for what's left is *anatta,* "no-self." Sri Ramana Maharshi, in his Hindu vocabulary, would say we've realized the fundamental identity of *atman* (individual self) with Brahman (boundless, universal Self). Sufis might say we've lost ourselves in the intoxicating presence of the Divine Beloved. Christians might say we've attained rapturous communion with the Holy Spirit. In plain-vanilla American, we might say we've noticed that we're simple Being, radiant Is-ness, rather then a thing that is.

But the liberating reality of who's there is nonsectarian and indescribable. Not through words but through practice (and luck or grace) do we get down to the joyous actuality of the Unnamable. All words on this topic (including these, of course) are ultimately misleading—just more names for us to crack open.

Knock-knock.
Who's there?
God.
God who?
God knows.

SUGGESTIONS FOR FURTHER PRACTICE:

- Another method of self-inquiry is to gaze at "yourself" in the mirror. Or sit with a partner and gaze into each other's eyes. Don't try to see or experience anything in particular, don't try to communicate anything, don't try to be "spiritual," and don't make it a staring contest: just relax, open your gaze, and let whatever happens happen. If the sense of clearly defined, separate selfness seems somehow to soften and melt, fine.

I'm nobody. Who are you?
Are you nobody too?
—EMILY DICKINSON

4. Eh...What's up,(Doc?

"B UGS" MEANS CRAZY. "Bunny" means baby rabbit. Bugs Bunny is neither. What's up with that?

Bugs is crazy like a fox—he's elusive prey. In cartoon after cartoon he faces certain death at the hands of the mighty hunter Elmer Fudd; but, bunnylike, he's perpetually born again. He's an Easter bunny, ever resurrected out of each hopeless situation. He keeps going and going and going . . .

The most elusive of prey is the Spirit, truth, enlightenment, God, and we're the hunters. He taunts us: **Eh . . . What's up, Doc?** But even with all our Doc-torates (is Ph.D. pronounced "Fudd"?), with our Elmer craniums grotesquely swollen with knowledge (yet naïve, baby-bald), we can't catch him. There's more in heaven and earth than is dreamt of in our philosophy. Elmer is clueless, he flunks the koan, he *never* knows what's up.

He's too caught in hunger and blood lust—our overheated intellect crashes repeatedly against the infuriatingly cool nonchalance of the Bugsy truth.

Bugs's koan starts with **Eh**, an all-American mantra evoking the pause before formless awareness concretizes into words and thoughts: the wisdom of uncertainty, omnidirectional openness to all possibilities (they multiply like rabbits), the child-mind that is required to enter the kingdom of heaven, the bunny-innocent tabula rasa (with voice by Mel Blanc). Then follows the challenge: **What's up?** What's the story? What's reality?

But also: Define your frame of reference; defend your dualities; show you know which end is up. Up and down, two of the earliest, most unequivocal absolutes we learned as children, turn out to have only relative, earthbound meaning. "Up" is away from the center of the earth, opposite gravity's pull. But when Bugs defies gravity and walks on ceilings, that concept melts down. From an expanded, deep-space perspective, which way is up? We picture the earth with the North Pole at the top, and then set the universe This End Up. But who put north at the tops of maps but our own Fuddy-duddy conceptual mind? Since its whole world is constructed of such dualities (up and down, yes and no, male and female, fair and foul, alive and dead), dat wascally wabbit has wecked evwything.

We cwucify people who do dat. ("Kill da wabbit, kill da wabbit!") But only to commune with them, assimilate them, cook and eat them as rabbit stew and so absorb their secret knowledge. We want the miraculous creativity and the conquest of logic and physics whereby Bugs conjures endless mallets and anvils out of the nonexistent pockets of his nonexistent pants. We want the magical power of self-renewal whereby he shape-shifts into Humphrey Bogart in a trench coat, Carmen Miranda in a fruit hat, or, most disconcertingly, Elmer himself. Bugs is the master of the ultimate magic trick, the rabbit who continually pulls himself out of his own hat. But, devout carnivores, we insist on cooking him for second-hand spiritual protein, grazing for immortality at the top of the food chain. It never occurs to Elmer to skip the middle-rabbit and eat a carrot, Bugs's elixir of power—to emulate the shaman instead of sacrificing him. If only Elmer would leave off hunting for a moment, he would see golden carrots in abundance, free for the taking, a universe of carrots sprouting like the lilies of the field.

In another incarnation, Bugs is the Road Runner, the bird that runs as free as if it were wheeling across the heavens, even as it navigates the roads of earth. Then Elmer is Wile E. Coyote, too wily for his own good, ever hoist with his own petard, catching only himself because concepts can catch only concepts . . . that's all, folks! Still the mind hungrily hunts the Road-Running no-mind, and can't catch it even with its cleverest devices, the very Acme of our ingenuity.

In another incarnation, Bugs is the fox in the song I sang as a child, to the tune of "The Farmer in the Dell":

A-hunting we will go,
A-hunting we will go,
We'll catch a little fox and put him in a box
And then we'll let him go.

We all try to keep that sly fox, that elusive Spirit, in some kind of box . . . confine that unconfinable Wild Thing within right angles and solid walls. The box is the mind. The box is a church.

The box is a book (this book, any book). God's in the box but doesn't fit; the Tao that can be spoken of is not the true Tao; the fox that can be boxed is not the true, wild fox. The Infinite is so vast that anything we say about it will be true. (Of *course* God's in our box—how can she be absent?) Also, the Infinite is so subtle that anything we say about it will be false. (Where'd she go?)

The fox is crazy like Bugs. He is crazy wisdom, and the crazy wisdom master. If we can catch hold of a teacher who embodies the Tao, the Light, the Unembodiable, we try to keep him boxed—keep him on the program, make him show up to lectures on time, package his teachings so they're logical and accessible, consistent and convenient. Lotsa luck. We're like tourists at the edge of the Grand Canyon, trying to capture its immensity in our little-boxy Kodaks. Smile!

To learn anything we need structure. To catch the Spirit, we need boxes. But to not kill the Spirit, we need to poke some air holes in the box. Then let him go/catch him/let him go/catch him/let him go. Put him in a box each moment, let him go each moment. This is the secret of the structureless structure, the effortless power, the powerful ease of all the foxy masters, from Bugs to Buddha, from B. B. King to the King of Kings.

We try to make sense of life, but life is beyond sensible—it's Bugs. As Elmer, we're determined to bag the meaning of it all, but it all means **Eh . . .** We go a-hunting for some ultimate state, but the Ultimate defies all states. After all our dogged pursuit, we don't finally reduce life to a formula; we awake to its being irreducible and nonformulaic. Like a hound after its prey, we keep thinking we've got it this time, but again it springs ahead. The quick brown fox jumps over the lazy dog.

• What's "up"? Images are projected upside-down on our retinas; their right-side-upness is purely a habit of interpretation. As you walk, look "down" at your feet and see your body extending away from the earth. Are you really projecting "up," like a stalagmite, or hanging "down," like a stalactite? It's all point of view. Now shift to the opposite view. Now shift to *no* view.

• Now try doing the same with other pairs of opposites: beautiful, ugly . . . masculine, feminine . . . foolish, wise . . . good luck, bad luck . . . future, past . . .

5. What's black and white
and red all over?

Q. What's black and white and red all over?
A. A newspaper.

✳

ALL NEWSPAPERS ARE pretty much inter-
changeable. Tension in the Middle East, scandal in
Washington, brushfires in California, floods in Bangladesh, the
Dow went down and up, Doc. Same script, different day. Yet,
with so many interweaving plot lines incrementally advancing,
the news is also an enticingly complex soap opera ("As the World
Turns," indeed), each episode somehow requiring our vicarious
involvement. Newspapers can be a seductive distraction, heating
us up, like pornography, into a fantasy state of virtual participa-
tion. As we squint at their narrow columns of print, the hibiscus
outside our window blossoms and dies, the glories of God or ac-
tuality-in-the moment dance unheeded.

Read not the Times; read the Eternities.
—THOREAU

But almost anything that can be done in a way that constricts our awareness can be done in a way that expands it instead. The Dalai Lama gets up at four o'clock each morning for two hours of prayer and meditation. Then he turns on his TV and, over breakfast, catches the news from around the world. How do those same floods and scandals resonate within the heart-mind of a being so wise and compassionate? How would we make the internal adjustment to experience the news as he does? Reading the morning paper is a daily opportunity to either reinforce our most deluded mental patterns or shatter them—a conscious opening of the heart or an oblivious closing.

What's black and white . . . ? The world is a place of richly nuanced tones and colors. Unless we're careful, the news becomes a reducing filter for rendering it into black and white: good guys (the ones who look and think like us) vs. bad guys (the others) in conflict over Great Issues That Really Matter.

> *Tweedledee and Tweedledum*
> *Agreed to have a battle,*
> *'Cause Tweedledum said Tweedledee*
> *Had spoiled his nice new rattle.*
> —LEWIS CARROLL

Presidential elections, wars and rumors of wars, the rise and fall of empires—viewed from a sufficiently cosmic perspective, they're all an infantile quarrel over an allegedly spoiled rattle. ("The nations are as a drop of a bucket, and are counted as the small dust of a balance." —Isaiah 40:15) And note that Tweedledum and Tweedledee *agree* to have a battle. Even the fiercest of combatants cannot engage in combat without a tacit agreement to so engage. From colliding planets to warring nations to interspecies predation, all conflict is a dance made specially exquisite by the dancers' refusal to acknowledge that it's a dance.

But it takes two to tango, even if they're as indistinguishable as Dee and Dum. Since we can't tell the players without a scorecard, the news industry supplies the stats we need to figure out that Dum is the home team (yay) and Dee is visiting (boo). Stories with multiple players of dubious moral standing bore and unsettle us—we turn the page quickly. We crave players in black hats and white hats, like the cowboys who slugged it out on the (black-and-white) TV's of my childhood.

Once we've decided who's black and who's white, we've earned the right to turn **red all over**—inflamed with the intoxicating passion of what we now call our "opinion." It's so sweet to know that our opinion is right and others are wrong. If only we were President, we'd straighten everything out; then everyone would see how right we are. Never mind the many times we turned out to be wrong, when the President did well to ignore the advice we shouted at the TV screen, or did poorly by taking it.

But even if we had the perfect prescience to be always miraculously right, that would just be a more seductive form of mental bondage. There's a point where we'd rather be free than right, where we don't care what other people think anymore because we don't care what *we* think, where we find the courage to Just Say Hmmmm, to liberate ourselves from black-and-white thinking. Opinionating at last becomes too cheap a high, too crassly sweet a confection. It starts to feel toxic, and it's time to kick.

Do not seek for truth—merely cease to cherish opinions.
—THIRD ZEN PATRIARCH

From opinionating, it's a short step to judging: exalting the good guys and condemning the bad. Jesus says that shouting "You fool!" (while seeing red?) is a sin—that is, it's one of the ways we evict ourselves from the kingdom of heaven within, close ourselves off from blissful openness of awareness. Condemnation and exaltation are overlays, projections of our own dualistic minds, which keep us from seeing the nondual reality underneath. You can fetch me a quart of milk or a pound of sugar, but you can't show me a quart of good or a pound of bad. Even a unanimous projection (Hitler is bad) is still a projection.

But dualism is so *satisfying.* It's such fun to root for the home team, for the saints and against the sinners. All a ticket to that game costs us is our self-knowledge. We have only to diligently avoid asking whether *our* hat is black or white: the inevitably gray answer spoils our fun by implying that everyone else's must also be gray. The diabolic child molester was once an angelic molestation victim. As the wheel of time spins, victim equals molester equals victim equals molester—it's all a blur. We're all more or less the same mix of desires and frustrations, ideals and resentments, lucid insights and dumb miscalculations, profound joy at being alive and acute embarrassment at living in a sporadically leaky, smelly animal body. And looked at even more closely, we're all pure Existence, all God: by definition, the Omnipresent must be everywhere, everything, every*one.*

Does nonjudgment mean, then, that we take no action against the Hitlers of the world? Not at all. Hamlet's discovery that "There is nothing either good or bad, but thinking makes it so" is what eventually frees him to take arms against his own Hitler, King Claudius. Only when he stops measuring himself against absolute good can he move against relative bad. "Judge not, that ye be not judged" means that when we place a black hat on another, we're stuck with a white hat ourselves, and it never fits.

By renouncing such judgment, Hamlet liberates himself from his paralyzing doubt about his own worthiness to act. He grows up. Real grown-ups don't need cartoon villains to make them feel like cartoon heroes; they just do what they have to do, which may include restraining those who cause suffering. But that's not how they get their kicks. Everyone's a sleeping buddha, but some are walking in their sleep, knocking things over, injuring others as they flail about in their feverish nightmares, and sometimes we may have to smack them into submission; with luck, we may even smack them a little more awake. We can afford to do this only as long as we maintain our reverence for them as buddhas. Thus Islamic tradition venerates Ali, the Prophet's beloved son-in-law, who spared an enemy soldier on the battlefield because he could not kill him without anger.

Black and white is "knowledge of good and evil," the dualistic perspective that expels us from the Garden in which all is Brahman—pure, luminous, nondual Being. Once we bite that red apple of judgment, it flavors and colors everything; then we live in a black-and-white-and-red-all-over world. Everything is viewed through the twin distorting lenses of aversion and attraction, and we're condemned to work ourselves red in the face (getting our bread by the sweat of our brow) to fight the bad and run after the good.

But there are ways back into the Garden. By relinquishing

judgment, by viewing everyone as sacred incarnation, by perfecting that view through meditative and devotional practice, we
can let mind melt into its own inherently spacious, worldless,
newsless nature.

*The real news inside here
is there's no news at all.*
—RUMI

And then we can find compassionate ways to welcome others
into the Garden with us. We can even invite them to join us as
we bask in its luxuriance, sit back in our garden chairs, and read
the morning paper.

SUGGESTIONS FOR FURTHER PRACTICE:

• Read news as history, or anthropology. As if you were a
visitor from the twenty-third century or from Neptune, read
about the struggles of Democrats and Republicans in the
same disinterested way we read now about Federalists and
Whigs.

• If you are a liberal, buy a copy of *Commentary* or *The National Review;* if conservative, *Mother Jones* or *The Nation.* For
an hour or two, suspend your beliefs and attitudes and enter
wholeheartedly into the perspective of the magazine you are
reading. (Adapted from Robert Anton Wilson)

• Cut out a news photo of your favorite loathsome bad guy.
Place it alongside a picture of your favorite transcendental
good guy—the Buddha, the Blessed Virgin, your guru, etc.

Each day, as you light your incense or say your prayers, acknowledge that the same divine light shines through both. (Adapted from Ram Dass)

• Go cold turkey. For a week or a month read no news whatsoever. Mute the TV when news briefs come on. Avert your eyes from headlines. Note how you feel, what you miss, whether the world seems to get on without you. When you go back to reading the news, note whether it still grips you as intensely as before.

• Read the news through the eyes of the buddha that you fundamentally are. Gently relinquish any judgmental or vindictive responses that (your intuition tells you) a buddha does not harbor. Gently enlarge upon your compassion for all who suffer.

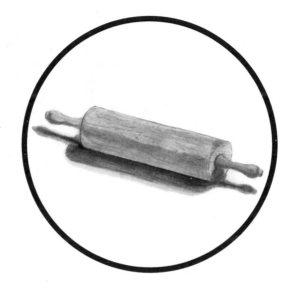

6. Take my wife...please!

*G*LORY TO THE great Henny Youngman, World's Fastest Comedian, King of the One-Liners, Venerable Sage of the Borscht Belt, who plays the inaudible music of the spheres on his incongruous violin. In this, his most famous teaching, Roshi Youngman employs the classic Zen method, shifting the ground beneath the student's feet from the conceptual to the actual, from abstract theory to concrete, compassionate experience. This superconcentrated joke pivots on the word **Take**, which we hear at first in its theoretical sense, as if a hypothetical premise were being presented. Then, in one blindingly swift instant—in one word, one syllable—all abstraction is blown away by the revelation of a real plea from someone in real pain: **please** take her.

Life, we suddenly see, is not a thought but an experience, within which suffering beings await our aid. Every time we think we've got life reduced to a safe, tidy model, it presents us with something that doesn't fit, something that may hurt. For philosophers and seekers who dwell in the realm of the abstract, this wake-up call from the concrete may come in the person of the spouse—the husband, or, in this case, **my wife.** Domestic frustration and misunderstanding can plague even the most profound philosopher.

A prophet is not without honor, save in his own country, and in his own house.

—MATTHEW 13:57

. . . and a guru is not without disciples, save in his wife's kitchen. Legend has it that Socrates lived in a state of tranquil philosophical harmony with everything in the universe but his wife Xanthippe. This is not a catastrophe, but a crucial function of life/wife: again and again, to knock our theoretical model to bits and make us see beyond our elegant hypotheses. (With one deft swipe of the rolling pin, she refutes them all.) In that sense the spouse *is* the guru. We are invited to look into our relationship, even (or especially) if it's a stormy one, and see how it can become a passage to deeper realization.

Still, there may be a point where it makes sense to take shelter from the storm, to live the life without the husband or wife. Celibate single life can also be highly conducive to the pursuit of enlightenment; most traditions boast great enlightenment heroes who were renunciates. But many were not. (The Buddha famously abandoned his wife and child. Jesus may well have been married; there is no historical evidence that he was or wasn't.)

The benefit of single life is largely pragmatic—it leaves more time for formal spiritual practice. Particularly in ages past, when most people scratched out a difficult living, tilling their fields or managing their cottageful of kids from sunup till sundown, one couldn't devote a day, no less a year, to uninterrupted meditation without renouncing family life and worldly occupations.

But nowadays, especially in the more affluent societies, we have roomier living quarters and shorter work weeks. If we take advantage of them, most of us have the space and time to do some serious inner exploration without moving to a cave. It's helpful to notice how we use whatever silent solitude is available. Do we fill it with habitual distractions (turning on the radio the moment we start the car, grabbing a magazine whenever we go to the bathroom), or do we dive into it?

Even so, there are spiritual advantages to single life, for those suited to it, whether in a monastery or a condo. There are longer stretches of silence to dive into, and one's devotional impulses are free to focus one-pointedly on the Vast One. Also, our sexual energies have deep, usually hidden connections to some of our most powerful attachments (such as our sense of security) and emotions (such as rage). There can be great value in taking time to cool off and clarify these energies—a process that happens not through intellectual analysis but by settling into the simplicity of Being. Even if we're carrying confusion or pain that is deeply tangled, it can come untangled as we reconnect with a silence that is deeper still.

After ten years in the red-light district,
How solitary a spell in the mountains.

I can see clouds a thousand miles away,
Hear ancient music in the pines.

—IKKYU

Appreciation of celibacy's refreshing spiritual benefits, though, has sometimes degenerated into the view that sex is somehow "bad" or "sinful." Churches can turn what should be a joyous expression of aliveness into a snakepit of guilt, and monasteries can become havens of neurotic repression. Still, that doesn't detract from the real value of genuine renunciation. In any case, celibacy in its highest form (whether practiced for a month or a lifetime) is more an *effect* of spiritual growth than a cause; it's more about not needing any than not getting any. This is the state of blissful self-sufficiency, where "they neither marry, nor are given in marriage; but are as the angels which are in heaven." This is effortless freedom, where we don't feel compelled to indulge *or* abstain. Bonking your brains out is just not so urgent an issue when your brains are nirvanically blown out already. Merging with another body is wonderful, but it's not so crucial when you're already merged with the transcendental No-body.

SUGGESTIONS FOR FURTHER PRACTICE:

• Occasionally, renunciation of *any* pleasure can be an effective tactic for relativizing its hold on us. If handled gracefully, renunciation can loosen the whole complex web of desire and fulfillment, helping us see That which lies outside the web. The technique is simple. Just as you're about to fulfill a desire—the ice cream carton is open, the scoop is in your hand—let it go instead. Breathe out, put the ice cream back in the freezer, and move on to the next order of business.

• There may also be times when it's useful to give something up for an extended period (say no ice cream for a year), although sometimes renouncing sneakier, more subtle indulgences (say, a particular form of self-righteousness or exhibitionism or inhibitionism) may be more important.

Many traditions incorporate this practice, but people often forfeit the real benefit by continuing to hold on. ("I stopped smoking for Lent, and I'd do anything for a cigarette"; "I'm fasting for Yom Kippur, and I'm dying for a sandwich.") To give up a thing means to hand it *up* (to God, to the Void); if you're still holding on to it, you haven't *given* it. Take my ice cream, Lord . . . please.

• When you're celibate, it's important to regard your celibacy not as a noble sacrifice or as a down payment now for heaven or buddahood later, but as a privilege—as part of your celebration of the radiant present moment. When you're not celibate, you can regard your lovemaking in exactly the same way.

7. Why did the chicken
cross the road?

Q. Why did the chicken cross the road?
A. To get to the other side.

✳

HIS IS THE great American koan of self-transformation. This is the great riddle, the supreme riddle, the White Whale and Everest of riddles. With archetypal precision, it pulls the rug out from under the mind, propelling it into a pratfall, a momentary flight that defies our usual, carefully maintained gravity. The question bamboozles us into expecting a specific, rational, purposeful answer: The chicken crossed the road to flee the fox, to search for chicken feed, to file his tax return, to register for classes, to mount a good-looking hen. We are lulled by the word **Why**, by our own sleepy assumption that all actions must have purposes, that shit (even chicken shit) don't just happen.

But then the answer ambushes us awake, annihilating our expectations. We are blown into the nonrational, purposeless Void—**the other side.** The question is just a question, but the answer is primal Mystery. It goes beyond funny to the essential, subversive Fun of purposeless, self-sufficient Being. For a moment the fabric of rationality is torn; we laugh as we fall through into the underlying Awareness-Space, whose nature is Great Bliss. *Whoops . . . Ahhh!* This fall, however it may be precipitated, is the One Joke that makes Rumi smile, Buddha laugh, and Jesus raise his cup.

The road most people are on—or at least think they're on—is the sleek freeway of achievement, of straight-ahead linear motion toward some hypothetical ideal time and place somewhere up yonder, some well-lit, clearly marked turn-off to the Promised Land of success and/or retirement. But a few of us choose the dirt of the off-road, the roadless road that crosses the road. We're always a minority, those of us who dare to dart between the axles of the eighteen-wheelers of progress. They've got the manpower and they've got the horsepower. Let's go, troops. Whatsa matter . . . chicken?

To **cross the road** we'd better have a good idea of its topography. It runs arrow-straight from Point A to Point Z: life paths, career tracks, mortgage amortization schedules, along which drivers hurtle in the speediest vehicles their credit can buy, racing toward the Good Life. But our mission is not to cross the Bourgeois Taxpayer Lifestyle Turnpike only to turn onto the Bohemian Alternative Scenic Route—that would merely be to replace one road with another. We're talking about cutting perpendicular to the time-space axis of *all* relative activity. To cross *that* road we must make a very hard left (sound of screeching brakes, smell of burning rubber). We must take a new angle, ninety degrees to (at cross-purposes with) the entire worldly world. We must make the sign of the cross, not in a merely symbolic, sectarian way, with our hands, but with our very lives, with our tracks, where our rubber meets the road. We must hang out on that cross where the horizontal highway of finite doing intersects the vertical skyway of infinite soaring.

But why a **chicken**? This most proverbially domestic, most pathetically flightless of fowl, unlovely of feather, unmelodious of song, exists (the dumb cluck!) only to eat and be eaten. The chicken is an unreflective, inexpressive machine for turning corn into white meat. This is precisely the role commercial society assigns *us* if we let it: producer-consumer-commuters, shuttling between job (where we are subject to the pecking order) and home (where we struggle to rule the roost).

So, relinquishing the safety of our familiar pecking ground and the secure numbers of the flock, let us look both ways and cross the road. The danger, we have been promised, is temporary. There's a famous Zen saying:

Before satori, mountains are mountains, valleys are valleys. While gaining satori, mountains are no longer mountains, valleys no longer valleys. But after satori, mountains are again mountains, valleys again valleys.

When everything goes topsy-turvy, Chicken Little thinks the sky is falling. But once we **get to the other side**, things get put back together again. Neophyte spiritual seekers are sometimes surprised to learn that seasoned spiritual finders live outer lives that are thoroughly conventional, that highly realized lamas may watch "The Simpsons" and eat Big Macs. ("In fact, the higher we go, the more we come down to earth."—Chögyam Trungpa Rinpoche) It's only during that tricky in-between, road-crossing phase that the things of the conventional world—jobs, relationships, objects, feelings, thoughts during meditation— seem to pose some sort of threat. Before that we're oblivious, happy birds, content to keep our heads down and peck. Afterwards we're enlightened free-range Superchickens, soaring with ease over all kinds of traffic.

Some people—especially the Holden Caulfields and Franny Glasses of this world, the sensitive, questioning spring chickens— have already boldly abandoned the safety of the flock without a clear vision of what's on the other side. Seeing the conventional world as the great enemy of their freedom and integrity, they may seek to overthrow it, either on the macro scale through radical activism, or on the micro scale through radical lifestyles. When they first discover spiritual practice, they often choose the most world-denying, renunciate path they can find. They're not necessarily wrong; it may be an appropriate strategy for that phase of their development.

But as our awareness grows, as inner freedom and integrity become unshakable, the world ceases to be a threat.

> *The infinitely diverse structures of relativity, far from being some dangerous disease, are actually a healing medicine. Why? Because in their intrinsically selfless nature, interdependent structures perfectly express the mystery and transmit the spiritual energy of universal friendliness.*
>
> —PRAJÑAPARAMITA SUTRA

As we come to enjoy that universal friendliness, we may appreciate what a clever dodge conventional living is. There's nothing like a regular haircut and a nondescript suit of clothes to give you a nice, comfortable perch from which to enjoy the most radical modes of awareness. (*Radical* means "at the root"—if we're wild at the root, painting wild colors on our leaves becomes optional.) As we grow in our clarity of cognition, we come to see that the crystalline, mirrorlike nature of our awareness can reflect all colors without ever becoming any of them. Eventually nothing, no matter how comfortable or uncomfortable, can impinge on our freedom. (How about the soft leather seat of a gold Cadillac under your butt? How about nails through your hands?) Mountains are once again mountains. Everything's just the same as before.

Only different. Because now we're seeing it from the other side. We still see cars zipping along the turnpike (we don't lose the world of linear activity; enlightenment does not equal coma). But viewed from the other side, they're going the other way; now traffic that once flowed from our left to our right goes right to left. Jesus describes this reversal precisely: "Many that are first shall be last; and the last shall be first." We are correct in understanding this as a reversal of rich and poor, success and failure, zooming Porsche and stalled Yugo. But misapplying the road logic of time and space, we might guess that Jesus is prophesying a radical reordering of society up around the next bend of the future. He's actually reporting something much more profound: a radical reordering of perception in the present. Beyond loss and gain, clear of all traffic, he has attained the permanent Free Parking space (along with Buddha and Mira and the rest of his friends—he claims no Monopoly).

This crossing over to the new world, this journeying to the

far shore of same-but-different, is evoked in one of the most powerful sound-vibration formulas of Mahayana Buddhism, the Mantra of Transcendental Wisdom:

Gaté gaté paragaté parasamgaté bodhi svaha!
Gone, gone, supremely gone, supremely totally gone, awakened—
wow!

With mantra, as with poetry, the sound is at least as important as the meaning; or, rather, the true meaning is the reality that we experience by immersing ourselves deeply in the sound. It is said that every time this mantra is written, read, chanted, or heard, all beings everywhere are helped in reaching that far shore of enlightenment, of ultimate Reality.

But how do we know there *is* another side to get to, that we're not recklessly jaywalking for naught? Until we've had enough experience to know for sure first-hand, there is the testimony of those who've crossed before. Unless Jesus and Buddha and Shankara and Chuang-tzu and Kabir and St. Teresa and Moses and Yeshe Tsogyal and Plotinus are *all* grievously mistaken, there's something over there. And even without reliance on rumors, we may intuit the answer. A front implies a back; a side implies another side. If I find a dime heads up, I assume that flipping it over will reveal the tails side that was hidden. If I find existence unsatisfactorily limited, I at least suspect that flipping it over will reveal a satisfactory limitlessness.

There is a reward for those willing to put themselves on the line, to commit their lives to a direction that has nothing to do with anything measurable, reasonable, or socially rewarded. "Whosoever will lose his life for my sake shall find it," says Jesus.

We *do* graduate. Once we've made that perilous crossing of self-transformation, we're no longer chicken—we've shown our pluck. No longer preyed-upon food-fowl victims of time-space, we are magnificent predators, rapturous raptors, swooping down upon and eating up the world of mundane experience, transmuting it into pure, soaring vision.

Ironically, then, chickens never get to the other side. By the time they arrive, they've become the Eagle of the Lakota, which soars above the animal nations of the four directions, carrying the pipe prayers to Grandfather Sky . . . they've become the Spirit in the form of a dove, which descends upon the man Jesus and makes him the enlightened Christ . . . they've become Big Bird, inviting us all to come and play where everything's A-OK . . . they've become the Garuda of the Hindus, who is the mount of God, the vehicle that conveys the divine Reality simultaneously everywhere . . . they've become the other Garuda, the Tibetan space eagle, who devours the serpents of ignorance and who, between the wing of spacious wisdom and the wing of compassionate activity, spans the cosmos.

From that high-flying, cosmos-spanning viewpoint, all this talk of crossing roads and getting to other sides is just a trick of dualistic language—a joke, indeed. We never go anywhere. Whatever we're experiencing in the present moment, *this* is the far shore, if only we can open ourselves to it completely. The Promised Land is not some external piece of real estate toward which we journey through space, or even some internal state of enlightenment for which we strive in time. *This is it.*

This world is the City of Truth, its maze of paths enchants the heart:

*We can reach the goal without crossing the road, such is the sport
    unending.*

—KABIR

*Seymour once said that all we do our whole lives is go from one
little piece of Holy Ground to the next. Is he never wrong?*

—J. D. SALINGER

Gaté gaté turns out to be not a request but an affirmation, a celebration; it means gone, gone, beyond the illusion that there's
anywhere else to go.

Q. Why did the Garuda cross the universe?
A. Here we are!

Sacred
Nursery
Rhymes

8. *Ring around the rosy*

Ring around the rosy,
A pocket full of posies.
Ashes, ashes,
We all fall down.

✳

RING AROUND THE Rosy," passed down from child to child in a game that is an ancient rite of initiation, celebrates the realization that our lives revolve around a central mystery. Through this ritual our culture ensures that every child knows, as Einstein put it, that something deeply hidden has to be behind things. The rumor that this rhyme describes the Great Plague of London—with rings drawn around rose-colored rashes, herbs carried in pockets for magical protection, and corpses being burnt into ashes—is probably false, scholars say. In any case, the specific origins of the game have long since dissolved into the more universal resonances that keep children playing it.

Ring refers to the circle dance that accompanies the song. Together they reflect a truth expressed throughout the world in art and myth: *Our lives are not linear.* We like to believe we're marching in a triumphant straight line, but we're really going in

circles—so we may as well relax our martial stride and get down
with the dance. Most ancient cultures recognize this cyclic nature of life. Some call it the wheel of samsara and say we go
around not just once but countless times, birth after death after
birth after death. After all, *we're* efficient enough to recycle our
cans and bottles; might not the universe be efficient enough to
recycle us?

> *'Round and 'round and 'round you go.*
> —CHUCK BERRY

Perhaps, then, the meaning and fulfillment of our lives is to be
found not in some great culminating achievement at the end of
a path we travel in time, but at the center of the circle we dance
in eternity—right now.

What is in the center?

That's hard to say. In fact, it's impossible to say, because words
are a part of our orbital dance; like comets hurling themselves at
the sun, they burn up as they reach the center. They can, however, work by analogy. Life's central essence is certainly not, say, a
rose, which is merely a thing, a flower; but let's call it **the rosy**
because it is in some ways *like* a rose. A rose is beautiful. A rose
opens out from a central point into a complex, radial labyrinth (a
mandala) of petals. There is no "rose" separate from its petals; if
you peel them away, looking for the rose, nothing's left. But this
nothing that dwells somewhere among the petals gives off a
wonderful fragrance.

> *It's just nothing. But there's something very good about it.*
> —MAHARISHI MAHESH YOGI

This enticing, sweet-smelling, rosy quality—this hint that existence is, at its core, mysteriously, transcendently good—keeps us orbiting, as the sun's gravity keeps the planets, in a **Ring around** it. Like it or not, consciously or unconsciously, this pull is what our lives are about; so the song tells us.

Eventually the planets may be drawn right into the sun, but for now its centripetal pull is counterbalanced by a centrifugal force, begun in the dim past, that continues of its own momentum. We are simultaneously attracted to and repelled by the Sacred. Our primal desire is to merge with it, yet we keep choosing otherwise, choosing to distract ourselves from boundless fulfillment. If I opened myself to the full blast of the Infinite, what would happen to my grip on the finite? Would I become a babbling saint? A God-intoxicated madman? And then who would run my department, water my plants, check my stocks? We're afraid even to *look* at that central sun, terrified of flying into it. We'll do anything (we do everything) to keep from smelling that Rose, for fear that its astonishing perfume would render us unfit for the dance of daily routine, unable or unwilling to keep coloring inside the lines.

> *But let not God speak with us, lest we die.*
> —EXODUS 20:19

As a consolation prize, therefore, we get **A pocket full of posies**—humbler flowers, less spectacularly gorgeous, less sweet-smelling, something we can live with, something pocket-sized, small tokens of the power of that terrifying central beauty but stepped down to an amperage we can handle. We settle for less, for now. Every small joy carries with it whispers of a greater

Joy deferred. God smiles at us through the rainbow, but it's merely a hint of that deluxe Technicolor rainbow we rightly suspect we're refusing to see. This suspicion creates a shortage mentality: afraid we'll run out of beauty, out of bliss, out of love, we become posy scavengers. We're collectors, stuffing our pockets with possessions, sensations, memories, relationships. But a flower in your pocket always dies; the tighter we clutch things, the quicker we crush them.

He who binds to himself a joy
Does the wingéd life destroy.
—WILLIAM BLAKE

Whether our carefully maintained cache of prizes is a house full of art treasures, a heart full of nostalgic moments, or a mind full of epiphanies, it takes more and more work to wring less and less fulfillment out of them.

When at last we tire of all that work, we're ready for **Ashes, ashes**—the fires of destruction. **We all fall down.** Exhaustion and death are universal. Tragedy happens. We can't keep dancing forever—they shoot horses, don't they? In the Hindu system, this is the domain of Shiva, the great Lord of Dissolution. But Shiva is also the Lord of Transcendence, of dissolving into the essence. When we give up our noisy dance around the circumference, we embrace the silent center. The children tumble to the ground and worship that still point through imitation: this is the only time in the game when they become still also. Sleeping, dying, transcending—all forms of silence, all forms of surrendering doing into Being.

And then we get up. After sleep we awake; after meditation

we act; after death (so the ritual promises) we are in some way resurrected or reborn, to dance the ring dance once again. No child ever plays just one round of this game, falling down and leaving it at that. But traditional wisdom promises also that the wheel of samsara is not endlessly redundant. With each cycle of waking and sleeping or living and dying, we catch a clearer glimpse of that central Rose; after each falling down we carry a little more of that stillness back with us to our dancing orbits. We integrate Being into doing until realization is attained.

Words cannot convey the direct experience of that roseate mystery. But the great teachers gesture toward it in countless subtle or startling ways. They sing their songs and tell their jokes from widely distant points on the circumference. Then they leave us to infer, within our own wordless awareness, the center that is equidistant from all their words. Because of differences in culture and language and the shapes of our mouths and ears, the descriptions may sound contradictory. You can call it Brahman or you can call it Tao, you can call it Shunyata or you can call it Allah, you can call it Yahweh or you can call it nothing at all. A Rose by any other name would smell as sweet.

9. *Row, row, row your boat*

Row, row, row your boat
Gently down the stream.
Merrily, merrily, merrily, merrily,
Life is but a dream.

✳

M AYBE THIS IS just an innocent ditty—a catchy tune repeated so incessantly on the long bus rides of our childhood that we soon stopped hearing its silly words. But maybe those words contain a cosmically liberative message that impelled us to repeat it with the same devotion as the most pious "Hail Mary" or "Haré Krishna."

The opening words—**Row, row, row**—address one of life's most universal problems: its enforced, no-exit drudgery. Like Adam after the Fall, we must get our bread by the sweat of our brow, toiling in the fields beyond the Garden, where we each have our row, row, row to hoe. Like Sisyphus, we must roll, roll, roll our rock endlessly up the mountain.

What is it that we must row? **Your boat**—that is, your vehicle. The vehicle of our awareness is this boat we call the body, with all its frailties and demands: teeth that grow mossy without

frequent scrubbing; delicate immune system beset by insidious
germs; fragile bones in a world of speeding taxis; gastrointestinal
tract that requires a steady supply of dead remains of other beings plunged in at one end, indigestible remains of those remains squeezed out the other; nervous system that insists we
spend a third of our life swooned into stupor.

In this leaky boat we're rowing for our lives.

The vehicle is also our personality, that bundle of quirks that
we must schlep and be schlepped by through all our interactions—
our unique constellation of attachments and aversions, memories
and associations, opinions and prejudices, jokes and terrors. The
vehicle is also our home (rake the leaves, patch the roof, pay the
mortgage); it is also our car (change the oil, rotate the tires); it is
our job; it is the relentless business of living that must be attended
to no matter how tedious. Pass the salt, feed the dog, swat the fly,
raise the toilet seat, do your homework, attend your funeral, row
your damned boat.

But then, with the word **Gently**, comes the first hint of revelation. We must row, yes, but there's a way to do it lightly, without strain, to discharge all those duties gracefully. For this frail
vehicle is not the only thing that's moving. We float in something larger—**the stream**—and we can row **down** the stream.
And the existence of an upstream and a downstream implies
something larger still: an ocean toward which we are being carried, if only we'll stop struggling against the current. If we look
very closely, we may even see that all the circumstances of our
lives have been conspiring, from the beginning, to carry us
toward ocean-vast fulfillment and understanding.

That evolutionary direction is often obscured (especially

when we're temporarily foundering on the rocks), but it's always there, as we'll find out in the long run. Through the practice of surrender (in Arabic, *islam*) to our natural direction, we relax our proprietary grip on the oars and go with the flow. We still must row—we don't evade our work, but now our work *works*. Having realized that the direction of the stream is positive, we can actively cooperate with it. (Old Mr. Murphy goes to church every Sunday and prays: "Dear God, please let me win the lottery. *Some*one has to win it—why not me?" Over the years his pleas grow increasingly desperate. Finally, one Sunday the roof of the church opens up, a golden light pours through, and a thunderous voice proclaims: "Murphy! Murphy! Help me out! Buy a ticket!")

In the next line, the song melodically conveys the *experience* of rowing downstream. Having struggled fitfully up the scale for two lines, the melody suddenly descends—**Merrily, merrily, merrily, merrily**—in a luxurious delirium of ease. When we let the stream carry us oceanward, we get the growing taste of nirvanic bliss; each "merrily" reflects more joyous conviction. Thus, while novices often regard spiritual development as a grim business, the old yogis have a wonderful lightheartedness; they trip merrily along through life.

Eventually the good news overpowers the bad, with four **merrily**s to answer the three **row**s. (Four is the number of conclusive testimony: Four Noble Truths, Four Vedas, Four Gospels.) And the good news is: **Life is but a dream.** When we reach the ocean of *moksha*-liberation, nirvana, the kingdom of God, we find, to our infinite relief, that all that tooth brushing and oil changing and mortgage paying has no solid reality. It is merely Prospero's insubstantial pageant, such stuff as dreams are made of.

In Sanskrit this dream is called *maya*—literally "that which is not." Sri Shankara, the great ninth-century exponent of Vedanta philosophy, illustrates with the example of a deadly snake which, in better light, proves to be merely a piece of rope— nothing to run from, nothing to kill. "It is she [maya] who brings forth the whole universe." In the West, Shankara's rope is the Edensnake, with the endlessly complicated drama of toil and suffering it spawns: all shadow play. It's just a movie, man—just Plato's flickering images on the wall of a cave. Where's the burden of rowing our boat when neither boat nor stream nor rowing nor rower exists in any substantial way? It's but a dream, a trick of the light, a mental construct of our own devising. And once we know we've been devising it, we can start to stop, start rowing gently toward the ocean, where all dreams converge and end.

But how can life be but a dream? It's so . . . lifelike. Well, dreams seem lifelike too, while we're in them. Chased by the dream tiger, we're lost in realistic terror; caressed by the dream lover, we're lost in highly persuasive lust. Only when we wake do we say, "Oh, it was but a dream."

One who in dream sees things good and bad, high and low, favorable and fearful, thinks that they are actually real, and never for a moment thinks that they are unreal while dreaming. Even so is this world till the dawn of Self-Knowledge.

—Shankara

The sage Vasishtha said there are two kinds of dreams: the short ones and the long one. We call the short ones "dreams" when we wake from them each morning; we call the long one "reality" till we wake into enlightenment. The short dreams are really dreams within a dream. Each has its own self-validating logic, its own physics, its own built-in history. In dreams we may calmly watch our friends turn into giraffes, recalling that they've done that for years. For corroboration we can talk it over with them, look it up in books, measure and test with scientific instruments. Only when we awaken does the insubstantial pageant of dream friends, dream books, and dream instruments fade.

Similarly with Vasishtha's long dream. In the very next moment we may wake up, come downstairs to breakfast, and say, "Mom, I had the strangest dream. It seemed to go on for years. I dreamed I lived on a planet called—What was it? Urf? Urp? And the people there had only one head! And they didn't know how to photosynthesize, so they had to eat the remains of dead beings. (Could you pass the sunbeams, please?) And you won't believe how they reproduced!"

There can never be evidence for any "real" universe outside the mind; any such "evidence" is only one more experience within the mind. The finest low-comedy scene in the history of Western philosophy took place when Samuel Johnson confidently demonstrated the reality of the objective universe by kicking a rock. Where's the proof he is not kicking a dream rock with a dream foot to feel a dream impact? The great Tibetan yogi Milarepa, it is said, finessed a similar debate by passing his hand *through* the rock.

By challenging the reality of a dream, however, we may start to see through it. When we ask, "Wait, can people really turn into giraffes?" we somehow scratch against the fabric of the dream itself, wear it thin, and wake up; or, having realized we're dreaming, we can manipulate the dream, perhaps turn giraffes into hippos. Some spiritual traditions train their practitioners to engage in such lucid dreaming—"dream yoga"—as practice for challenging the reality of the long dream.

Once we know we're dreaming it all—that, even while running from the dream tiger, the dreamer himself is just having a nice snooze—then life, where is thy sting? Enlightenment is the lazy man's paradise. We literally do nothing; we realize we've always done nothing. This doesn't mean we become *outwardly* lazy. As long as we're *in* the dream, we do our best to make it a pleasant one. It's a dream reality, but we're really dreaming it. In fact, we may as well work away, since none of our work is substantially happening. We're on permanent vacation, having vacated the spot where we used to think we had a self, allowing all the work (all that rowing) to go on being done by the body and the personality we used to think we were. We are in the world but not of it; every thought, word, and deed is what Buddhists call "self-liberating." Thus, when asked how seekers of boundlessness can escape from such binding necessities as dressing and eating, Zen master Bokaju replied, "We dress, we eat."

Enlightenment doesn't mean we become a blissful vegetable parked somewhere in a cave, grinning and drooling, our diaper occasionally changed by devoted disciples. With nothing to gain from action, we perform actions that are pure, undistorted by the fear and hope spawned by belief in the dream. No longer slaves of maya (like the emaciated galley slaves in cartoons, driven by the whip and drumbeat of the burly rowing master), we can for the first time truly row *our* boat. In easy harmony with this downstream drift toward universality, we can relax into individuality. The awakened ones, far from dissolving their personalities into some bland kind of cosmic pablum, are more vividly individual than the rest of us dare to be.

Row, row, row: At first we row desperately, convinced that everything depends on it, and we're all alone in our little boat. Then we row gently, as we realize that something bigger is pulling us along. Finally, as we reach the ocean, the goal of all rowing, we row without rowing at all.

SUGGESTIONS FOR FURTHER PRACTICE:

- Until you've been trained in dream yoga, you can head in that direction just by holding the intention to be more aware while falling asleep, sleeping, and dreaming. Also, spend a little time each day regarding your waking experiences as a dream (but not while operating heavy equipment).

10. I'm a little teapot

I'm a little teapot, short and stout.
Here is my handle, here is my spout.
When I get all steamed up I will shout,
"Tip me over, pour me out."

✳

*J*LEARNED TO sing this song and mime a tipping
teapot in Miss Somebody's dance class, Westbury, Long
Island, circa 1954. (We also did the Froggy Dance, tune and lyrics
now lost to memory.) Now, forty-some years later, "I'm a Little
Teapot" summarizes our situation as we set upon the path of spiritual practice. Nothing has to be added to us, nothing has to be
changed—we just have to get turned right-side out. We already
contain the precious tea of limitless Existence; it has only to be
poured.

As we've seen, the "self" is a shaky construct at best. It exists
only as an infinite, transpersonal Self (the Hindu description), or
only in relation to God (Judeo-Christian-Islamic), or not at all
(Buddhist). No matter which description we prefer, it means
that any notion of the self as a distinct, limited, independent,
describable "thing" is only metaphoric.

Until enlightenment, we're just symbols of ourselves.
—NGAK'CHANG RINPOCHE

Symbols have their place, as long as we don't take them literally. For example, we may see ourselves as actors in a dramatic (sometimes melodramatic) movie, cast in a series of roles, usually auditioning for the flashiest ones. Such movie acting can be great fun unless we get lost in it. Then we have to live up to our roles, distort our behavior to stay in character, and constrict our vision to keep from being distracted by the wider world just beyond the edges of the movie set.

As long as we're living metaphorically, perhaps we ought to adopt metaphors that don't bind us so tightly, metaphors with a back door that opens onto the boundless Reality beyond all metaphor. So:

I'm a little teapot. "I" am just a utensil, a mere vessel. The structure that I usually call "me" is a humble object of secondary interest only, within which the object of primary interest—the essence, the hot stuff, the tea that is immortal nectar—is brewed. My outer structure, though, is paradoxical. Although I'm **short** along one axis (a being limited by time and space, body and personality), along another axis I'm **stout.** My chubbiness hints at the vastness of the formless substance brewing within the interior of my form. Traditionally, embodiments of vastness are often chubby: the elephant-headed Lord Ganesh of the Hindus, the pot-bellied Tibetan space eagle Garuda, Santa Claus, the buxom Venus of Willendorf, Seymour Glass's Fat Lady. Stoutness also implies strength, courage, perseverance—all qualities that will prove essential in escaping the limited concept of self.

Our structure also includes two special features that will help in this great escape. First, **Here is my handle**. No matter where we are in the world of samsara, no matter how deeply we're mired in confusion, no matter how remote help may seem, there is always some way to get hold of our situation and transform it—to get a handle on it. There's always a next evolutionary step, a process that is appropriate and available to this person at this moment. These processes are called *upaya,* "skillful means," and might include such traditional practices as meditation, yoga, scripture study, chanting, and prayer—all structured steps that lead us to structureless Being. But martial arts, counseling, body work, twelve-step programs, altruistic service, and relationships also can be upaya. Almost anything used in the right way at the right time may be a handle for grasping the otherwise too-hot-to-handle Reality. (This manifoldness of upaya is represented by the lavishly handled Avalokiteshvara, the Buddha of Compassion, who has a thousand arms.)

At some point, though, we may find that the do-it-yourself approach can get us only so far—that the handle is not strictly for our own use. After all, how can a teapot grasp its own handle? Only someone standing outside the vessel of limitation—a master or guru or lama, or God herself—can truly grasp it. The ponytails that devotees of Krishna wear are considered handles with which he hauls them into his transcendental realm. There comes a time when we have to let the teacher take hold.

Here is my spout. Our second special feature is the one through which we pour out our hidden inner riches, to get the tea that was inside outside. Jesus says, "Out of the abundance of the heart the mouth speaketh"—what we are is revealed in how we spout off. The voice is a crucial component in the process of gaining liberation. (Vajrayana Buddhists count three such components: body, voice, and mind.) We can use it to supplicate, to celebrate, to pray, to chant, to sing. We can and must use it to *express* (literally "press out") whatever is inside us—not just happy-face, have-a-nice-day "spiritual" sentiments. Most of us lug around carefully hoarded stores of secrets and evasions that needlessly weigh us down. Honesty is the best policy.

If you bring out what is inside you, what you bring out will save you; but if you do not bring out what is inside you, what you do not bring out will destroy you.
—THE GOSPEL ACCORDING TO THOMAS

This works even on the physiological level. The weight of all those secrets, the internal pressure of all that steam, creates stress, which in turn weakens the immune system. (Often when secretly HIV-positive children "go public," their T-cell counts go up.) Of course, compassionate common sense tells us we must be sensitive to the feelings of others in how and when we bring our various secrets out of the closet; but the reality is there's nothing to hide and no place to hide it. Once you realize God sees everything, it has been said, you're free. Everyone else probably sees it already anyway.

The spout, however, comes into play most especially **When I get all steamed up**—when I'm filled with anger, frustration, anguish, sorrow, dukkha. Something's got to heat up in our life to get us ready for awakening. Nothing much happens to the complacent; at some point we have to get steamed. There's an old joke about an apparently mute little rich boy. One morning at the elegantly set breakfast table, he says, "There's no butter on my toast." "You can talk!" exclaims his mother. "Of course I can talk." "Then why haven't you ever talked before?" "Up till now, everything's been okay."

In response to whatever kind of dukkha, whatever kind of unsatisfactoriness has me steamed, **I will shout**—I will call upon life or the Lord or the lama and register my heartfelt complaint.

> *The Lord is nigh unto all them that call upon him, to all that call upon him in truth.*
>
> —PSALM 145:18

Here at last the little teapot's sense of littleness turns out to be a blessing. The steam needs to build up pressure within the limited interior of the vessel before it can whistle; those who feel too big, too self-important, who have not felt the pressure of limitation, don't call for help. Too much butter on their toast.

After all, we are whistling for the guru to do something absolutely radical: to **Tip me over**. Upset my life, dear lama, disrupt my schedule, tear up my assumptions, make me crazy. When I was about to receive empowerment from Ngak'chang Rinpoche into a particularly high-octane spiritual practice, he warned us that not everyone in our group might want to learn it, because "it ruins your life." To illustrate, he gave the example of a chessboard to which just a few playing pieces—representing the elements of one's life directly conducive to realization—are bolted down. What the practice does, he explained, is to gradually tip over the chessboard till all the other pieces fall off. He once told the same thing to another group, in California. When they insisted, "Yes, teach us, ruin our lives," he said, "Okay—everyone meet back here at three A.M." "Oh . . . but that's so early . . . we'll be so tired the next day . . . it'll disrupt our schedule . . . it's so inconvenient . . ."

If, however, I can manage to cooperate with this chaos, the master will **pour me out**—free me from the confining walls of concepts, of secrets, of obscurations, of false notions of self, of everything. The bracing tea of enlightenment was always there, but hidden; she pours it out where it can be drunk. Actually, by examining any vessel—bowl, cup, teapot, cranium—we see that its walls merely create an illusion that the "inside" space is somehow divided from the "outside" space. If we move the vessel around, or break it, we see that there was always just one indivisible, boundless space. (How could space ever be divided from itself?) The illusion of boundedness is all the boundedness there is.

So, through diligent application of skillful means, and through the compassionate aid of masters who are always ready to help us (just whistle), we get outside the illusion of being inside. Our usual, unexamined picture of existence is that of an enormous universe containing countless galaxies, each containing countless stars; orbiting around one smallish star is a still smaller planet teeming with billions of very small people; one of those billions is me; and inside me somewhere—perhaps behind my eyes and between my ears—is a precious, tiny something, a "soul" or "spirit" or "awareness" or "self," like a flickering candle flame that I must carefully guard lest the forces of the enormous universe blow it out. This picture, the masters show us, is precisely inside out. Awareness is not a little flame or puff or droplet within a body within a universe. Our first clue is the simple fact that we're aware of our body—that the body is an object within awareness. Awareness is not within anything.

We are the limitless Awareness-Space within which bodies and universes arise and vanish. This realization is the right-side-outness we are determined to attain.

11. *Little Jack Horner*

Little Jack Horner sat in the corner,
Eating a Christmas pie.
He put in his thumb, and pulled out a plum,
And said, "What a good boy am I!"

✳

*O*H, MY. Here we are, stuck in **the corner**—cornered by life. It's all over, we're convinced; there's nowhere to go. Maybe it's our outer, objective circumstances that seem dead-ended: if only we could change our job, our marriage, our health. Or maybe it's our inner, subjective state: we're depressed, and even if we could change the externals it wouldn't help. Existence sucks. Life itself (we conclude in the depressed state) is inherently a bummer. Everything is flat and dry, we feel no joy or enthusiasm for anything, and (we're sure) we never will. It's not just that there's no light at the end of the tunnel. There's no such thing as light—there's nothing but tunnel.

Or corner. Now, whether the corner you're in is outer constriction or inner depression, stick with me. I swear there's a way out of here.

After all, who's keeping us in this corner? What angry Parent sent us here? For what transgression are we being punished? The rhyme doesn't say, we can't remember, and Jack Horner is **Little**, too young to have done any serious mischief. So the dead-end limitations of this life must be punishment for some kind of criminality we inherited, some congenital vermin we've been infested with since time immemorial. We've got . . . *the Cooties of Original Sin!*

But, *amartia,* the Greek word that is translated in the Bible as "sin," literally means "off the mark," as in the mis-shooting of an arrow. Period. Missing the mark is a valid, necessary part of any dynamic educational process, one component of the feedback system that leads us eventually to develop faultless aim. It's not a mysterious stain or blemish, virus or cootie, and it's not anything one can be born with. Sometimes the message of religions seems to have been reduced to "Oooh, you've got cooties!" and an offer to sell you their patented cootie spray— frequent refills required. But we're all immaculate all the time, because we're none other than the immaculate Infinite itself; we're perpetually absolved by the Absolute, which is our own ultimate identity. Even if we tried, there's no way we could ever stain it.

The fact is, nothing is keeping us in this corner except our own "mind-forged manacles." There's a story about a seeker who comes to a great master, throws himself at his feet, and cries, "O Master! Please cut the chains of ignorance that bind me." The master replies, "Show me your chains and I will cut them." We're peering so intently into the corner in which we think we're imprisoned that we don't notice we're already free. We don't have to change anything or go anywhere: just stay in the same spot and swivel. Just look *out* of our corner into the Vastness, reorient our awareness, take the reverse-angle shot, or, to use Jesus' term for turning ourselves around, "repent." But how? We'll see in a moment.

Speaking of Jesus, who's been sustaining us through this dark night? What has kept us going in this lonely corner? Jack has been **Eating a Christmas pie,** a Jesus birthday cake, the manna cooked up by Christ, Lao-tzu, Padmasambhava—pick your favorite divine pastry chef. Even without the full-course meal of his teachings, just the birth of such an extraordinary figure, just the savor of a savior, can change everything, can inspire us with the hope that we won't be sent to bed without our just desserts. And we can draw that inspiration whether or not we take these saviors' miraculous-origin stories literally. Christ's humble birth among the asses and oxen (a story that appears nowhere in the Bible, but survives because of its great symbolic power) promises us that even here, in this humble corner of our own beast-of-burden lives, redemption can be born. Lao-tzu's being sired by a shooting star promises us we are heirs to the power that spawns the brilliant cosmos. Padmasambhava's immaculate emergence from a lotus flower reminds us that our own true source, our own true nature, is ever-immaculate. But perhaps it's even more inspiring to guess that they were all just humans like ourselves, who somehow figured out how to get out of this corner. How extraordinary if they were perfectly ordinary.

> I am at once what Christ is, since he was what I am, and
> This Jack, this joke . . . is immortal diamond.
> —GERARD MANLEY HOPKINS

Perhaps, then, these saviors are fellow prisoners who have escaped and sent back a cake with a file in it. Or a pie with a plum.

He put in his thumb, and pulled out a plum: Here's the how-to part. The way out is in. To get to the outside, we have to explore the inside. Even though they're the finest bakers in the universe, we can't leave it up to Christ or Buddha or Shankara to hand us our liberation pie on a silver platter (or to hurl it, Stooges-style, in yo' face). We have to raise ourselves above those asses and oxen, take the initiative, and use our uniquely human opposable thumb—put it in, stick it out, and hitch our own ride through the galaxy. To pull out the plum, we must plumb the depths of that most precious gift, Existence itself; we have to do our meditative practice to reclaim the kingdom of God within; we have to break through life's crispy outer crust to relish the sweet squishy inner fruit.

Then we perceive our own basic goodness, free from limitation and shame, and we exult, **"What a good boy (or girl) am I!"** (This simple, fundamental goodness is what some people call "buddha-nature.") We cut the nonexistent chains of ignorance and become immune to the smooth spiel of flim-flam men hawking their cootie spray.

We're freed as well from the hell realm of the depressed state. *Enlightenment is the cure for depression.* Even the first glimmers of light caught in the first faltering steps of spiritual practice are enough to show that there *is* such a thing as light, and that can make all the difference.

> *Even a little of this dharma saves from great fear.*
> —BHAGAVAD GITA

Enlightenment, in a sense, is the opposite of depression; it is the state in which *everything* brings us joy and enthusiasm, and, we miraculously realize, always has and always will. Depression, it turns out, was a cracked-mirror reflection of enlightenment, a kingdom of hell whose agonizing pseudoeternity ironically foreshadowed the true eternity of the kingdom of heaven.

Please don't believe any of the voices, outer or inner, that say you're stuck in the corner called limitation, that joy has permanently fled, or that you're somehow worthless or "bad." Sooner or later you'll see the limitlessness which you are, in which you're sitting pretty, right now. You'll see what a good boy or good girl you are.

Suggestions for further practice:

- While enlightenment is ultimately the cure for depression, getting there can take a while. In the meantime, professional counseling may be indicated. Also singing in the shower (see "Hey, Hey We're the Monkees") and *abhyanga* (vigorous self-administered oil massage) for a few minutes before or after showering. It's also crucial to keep moving. Have a job, even if you have to make one up; get up every morning and go to it. Even if you feel that you're worthless and what you're doing is worthless, do it anyway. In cases arising from an excess of comfort and leisure, do volunteer work helping people with *real* problems. And dance, dance, dance.

12. *Mary had a little lamb*

Mary had a little lamb,
Its fleece was white as snow,
And everywhere that Mary went
The lamb was sure to go.

It followed her to school one day,
That was against the rule;
It made the children laugh and play
To see a lamb at school.

And so the teacher turned it out
But still it lingered near
And waited patiently about
Till Mary did appear.

"Why does the lamb love Mary so?"
The eager children cry.
"Why, Mary loves the lamb, you know,"
The teacher did reply.

✳

*T*HERE REALLY was a Mary—Mary Elizabeth Sawyer—and her little lamb really followed her to school, in Sterling, Massachusetts, one morning almost two hundred years ago. Decades later, Thomas Edison read "Mary Had a Lit-

tle Lamb" on his first cylinder recording, making it a kind of an-
cestor of every note and word recorded since. But why, out of
all the saccharine juvenilia of the nineteenth century, has this
poem been enshrined in the universal curriculum of childhood
wisdom? Close examination shows that it vividly describes the
mechanics of devotion—how focused love brings about spiritual realization.

Mary had a little lamb. All the silly parodies ("Mary had a
little lamb, / The doctor was astonished") point out the potent
double entendre of the word **had**, which amplifies the poem's
echoes of the Blessed Virgin Mary and her child, the Lamb of
God. By identifying her with an ordinary schoolgirl, the poem
makes the estate of the Virgin accessible to us, intimate, simple,
familiar. Walking with the Divine is as natural as walking to
school; as we grow in realization, we each give birth to the
Christ, to boundless perfect Being-Awareness. Then we are all
Mary, and all our conceptions are immaculate. From within the
womb of mind we bear our own redemption, the stainless,
lamb-gentle Redeemer.

Tibetans call this stainless awareness *sem karpo*—literally
"white mind," mind which has realized the immaculate "white-
ness" of the clear light of absolute Reality. Hence, **Its fleece
was white as snow.** Snow is water, the essence of life, but
frozen into crystalline mandalas whose macroscopic structure
amplifies and reveals the microscopic structure of each water
molecule. The radiant beauty of the snowflake is already present
in the water, merely awaiting the wintertime settling down of
thermal disorder before it displays itself, just as the radiant
beauty of Existence is already present in the moment, merely

awaiting the meditative settling down of the mind before it cog-
nizes itself.*

**And everywhere that Mary went / The lamb was sure
to go.** At the very end of the Gospel of Matthew, the Lamb of
God assures us, "Lo, I am with you always." This radiant
everything-perfect-as-it-is-ness never leaves us; by its nature, it
never *can* leave us. If we are Mary, the Lamb is flesh of our flesh.
We *are* Christ-consciousness, Buddha-mind. Wherever we go,
here it is.

> *Even when you feel you can't maintain that Awareness, be as-
> sured that it is maintaining you.*
>
> —LAMA SURYA DAS

**It followed her to school one day, / Which was against
the rule.** On one glorious day, the radiance that has been there
all along breaks through to the educated conceptual mind,
which till now has diligently filtered it out. Samadhi, nirvana,
Christ triumphant lays low all our concepts, breaks all the
rules: the rules of etiquette, the rules of physics, the rules of
grammar. It doesn't make sense, it doesn't make nice, it doesn't
make money. It overturns the tables in the Temple of rationality. It liberates us from the grinding wheels of cause-and-

---

*Hence *cool* is apt slang for that which is sublimely okay. The term was popu-
larized by the great tenor saxophonist Lester Young, the grandfather of cool
jazz (in which silence speaks louder than notes) and apparently the first person
to wear sunglasses as a fashion statement, to look as cool as he felt. In current
vernacular, the opposite of cool is *random,* which makes perfect sense: as a system's rate of random molecular activity increases, it heats up—it loses its cool.

effect lawfulness, concerning which we have been so exactingly schooled.

Love knows nothing of order.
  —ST. JEROME

This great liberation brings great joy. **It made the children laugh and play / To see a lamb at school.** Our entire life becomes laughing and playing, freed from the stern school-marms, the Miss Grundys of our own croaking, judgmental inner voices, who at first resist the Lamb of God and **turn it out.** Again and again the prophets are turned out—shunned, banished, jailed, committed, crucified. Again and again, we turn our faces from Eternity's sunrise to check the price of pork bellies, or turn up our car radios to drown out the deafening ecstasy of silence, or turn away from chances to reach out to one another in simple honesty and enthusiasm, retreating instead into numbing social ritual or defensive sarcasm. Again and again we glimpse the sublime vision of life as endless joy, only to be turned out, cast into outer darkness, with weeping and gnashing of teeth.

But that's okay too—that's the way it works. Something of the glimpsed vision is retained, and the totality of it hovers somewhere close by till we're ready to open to it again. **But still it lingered near / And waited patiently about / Till Mary did appear.**

Failing to fetch me at first keep encouraged,
Missing me one place search another,
I stop somewhere waiting for you.
  —WALT WHITMAN

Eventually even Miss Grundy cannot resist the charm of the Lamb. The schoolmarm is schooled by its unfailing love. To the question **"Why does the lamb love Mary so?"** she answers, **"Why, Mary loves the lamb, you know."** All the children (our fellow seekers and future fellow seekers—that is, everyone) will eventually see that liberation is for all of us, that Buddha-mind never abandons us, that Christ-heart loves us, and that what actualizes divine love on the human plane is human love.

> *He that loveth not, knoweth not God; for God is love.*
> —1 JOHN 4:8

> *Love is not an emotion; it is your very existence.*
> —SRI SRI RAVI SHANKAR

God is love is you, is the radiant openness that we find everywhere by finding the finder. We cultivate it in the focused form called *devotion*—devotion first to our parents and childhood friends and pets, then to our lovers and spouses, teams and ideals, gurus and gods.

> *I follow the religion of love wherever its camels turn.*
> —IBN AL-'ARABI

Eventually we discover that this love is our natural relationship with everything we encounter. We see how hard we used to work to obstruct our innate lovingness, and we let that Judas habit go.

Then there is no more turning out of the Lamb. The temporary bliss of samadhi becomes the permanent bliss of nirvikalpa samadhi. As Mary, the supreme pristine lover, we see that everything we behold is our very own Lamb of God. (Yes, sir, that's my baby now.) Each moment of experience is limitless natural beauty and joy, immaculately conceived in the womb of luminous awareness. We still have human personalities and tastes, even in enlightenment; so, with people as with music or movies, there are still some we like less or more than others. But we don't have to like 'em, just love 'em, and so we spontaneously do, with every breath and step, every burp and unsignaled left-hand turn. Then, in that white-mind state of sem karpo, our whole world comes exultantly alive as the gentle, loving, white-as-snow Lamb of God.

The mountains skipped like rams, and the little hills like lambs.
—PSALM 114:4

SUGGESTIONS FOR FURTHER PRACTICE:

• Consider deeply—not as an abstraction or a generalization, but as it actually applies to yourself—the poet Kabir's question: "Who is it we spend our entire life loving?"

• A very effective way to practice devotion is prayer—not necessarily in the sense of asking for anything, as devotion includes the understanding that everything is already given. Jesus suggests that the most profound kind of prayer (like all intimate meetings between lovers) takes place in private: "Go into your room and shut the door and pray to your Father who is in secret." One way to do this is to sit quietly, relax, and invoke the presence of the Radiant One by repeating the name God, Ram, Allah, Adonai, or whatever name touches you most deeply. Intone it as tenderly or vehemently as the moment requires (or defiantly, or despairingly, or accusingly . . . lovers have many moods). Of course, the One is *always* present—what you're really invoking is your *own* presence, enlivening and settling your attention in its omnipresence, opening yourself to its immediate actuality.

Don't try to "feel" this presence; don't seek or expect to feel *any* particular way; whatever you experience in each moment *is* that presence. After a while, leave off repeating the name. (Jesus cautions against the endless "heaping up" of repetitions.) Then just remain totally open to the Total Openness which God is. Rest in that; soak in it; marinate in it.

• If *no* name touches you deeply, or if you're more comfortable not giving the Unnamable a name, you're in good company. (Some of us swing both ways.) You don't have to wrestle with the logical problems of a creator deity; you don't have to reconcile the quirks of the divine Personality described in any particular scripture; you don't have to use any theistic name or form. Even exponents of Zen, perhaps the most purely nontheistic of paths, have declared for this ultimate love:

The highest reality is not a mere abstraction, it is very much alive with sense and awareness and intelligence, and, above all, with love purged of human infirmities and defilements.
                                                        —D. T. SUZUKI

All you have to do is open yourself to that Love with your love, to meet it on its own terms. One simple, nonsectarian method is the Seinfeld Prayer, derived from the episode in which Jerry becomes romantically involved with a woman whose name (to his embarrassment) he doesn't know. When she exclaims, "Oh, Jerry!" and passionately embraces him, he responds, "Oh . . . you!" Similarly, you can directly address yourself to that highest Reality, bypassing all doctrine, simply by saying, "Oh, You . . . You . . . You . . . " Or even skip the "You" and go straight to ". . . . ." Or you can use the Sanskrit exclamation *Namah!*—"I bow down!" You don't have to specify to whom or to what you bow down. From our side, it's the bowing itself that's important; the other side will take care of itself.

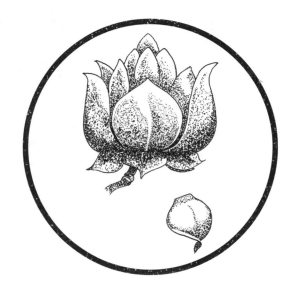

13. She loves me,
she loves me not

She loves me, she loves me not.
She loves me, she loves me not.
(Repeat)

✳

A SUFI FRIEND of mine used to take me to practice *zikr*—remembrance of God—in a mosque in SoHo that had been converted from an old firehouse. There, in a packed room that quickly grew warm, we formed concentric circles, each of us with one arm around the waist of the person on our right and the other over the shoulder of the person on our left. In this way we danced into the night, singing, over and over, *"La illa ha'illa'ellah!"* As we sang the first half of the mantra, *La illa*—"There is no God"—we turned our heads to the left, facing the possibility of a bleak, Godless universe. Then, just as we'd been completely plunged into this abyss, we turned our heads to the right, completed the mantra, *ha'illa'ellah!*—"but God!"—and experienced the exhilaration of rescue, of being pulled out of the abyss as quickly as we had been plunged into it. (These days, my son and I engage in a similar ritual watching basketball. As we turn our heads one way to watch the enemy team take the ball into their court, life is grim. When our team takes possession and we swing our heads the other way, life is full and good.)

She loves me, she loves me not, the traditional daisy-depetaling chant, resembles that Sufi mantra in both structure and meaning. The **she** who does or does not love me is, superficially, the human object of some school-yard infatuation. But from a vaster perspective she is also the capital-S She, the female aspect of divinity, the Mother, the giver of the shape of the universe. Then the chant asks a deeper question: Is God a loving Mother? Or is she an indifferent one—perhaps even a cruel Mommy Dearest? That is: Is life, by virtue of the cosmic principles that have given rise to it, beneficent, evolutionary, meaningful, loving? Or **not:** Is life at best neutral, merely mechanical, maybe even essentially a raw deal? Is the universe a closed system, ground down under the iron thumb of the Second Law of Thermodynamics, which dictates that, in time, things fall apart, entropy reigns supreme, all order turns to disorder, all structure turns to junk, life's a bitch (a bad Mommy) and then you die? Or is it an entropy-resistant open system, fed by some larger Reality that nourishes it even as the good Mommy nurses her child?

How can we know? In this chant, as we pull the petals off the flower just as we might count Hail Marys on a rosary, the answer lies in whether the number of petals is even or odd. The creator's signature, and hence her personality, is revealed in the mathematical structure of her creation: it's up to us to decipher the signature, like astute graphologists. But, surprisingly, **She loves me** comes out on the *odd* petal. We might have guessed

that an orderly universe requires an even number: every proton
has its electron, every cause its effect, every question its answer,
every Jack his Jill. But that would be to demand orderliness
within the closed-system universe, a simplistic symmetry custom-
made to flatter the closed-system intellect. We might just as well
demand that the stars be organized into tidy, symmetrical constellations, like the diagrams in elementary geometry books. Indeed, pathological perfectionism is only an extreme case of the
common desire to reshape the universe as docile ducks in a ster-
ile row.

But God the Messy, God the Odd, asserts her active, us-loving
presence by scattering our rows of ducks, slaughtering them if
necessary—whatever it takes to get our attention. In this aspect
she is Kali, Durga, Ekajati, the fang-baring, blood-drinking,
weapon-brandishing, skull-necklace-wearing Fierce Mutha'—
chomping and stabbing her way through our complacent expectations wherever her wrathful dance takes her. She guarantees
that we can't snooze along forever in some neat, even, self-
contained universe and never bother looking outside it.

In a Hindu story, some troublemaker grows tired of hearing
a holy man aver that all phenomena are the display of divine
beauty. He invites the holy man to supper and arranges things so
that, en route to his house, they encounter the putrid, rotting
corpse of a dog. "What a horrible thing to find on the street!"
the prankster says, watching closely for the holy man's reaction.
"Yes," he replies, "but look at its beautiful, pearly white teeth."
Even more precisely, in his realized state he sees that every cor-
puscle of the dead dog's blood and pus and entrails is pearly
beautiful. He has renounced the demand that a beautiful, or-

derly, loving universe include only healthy, photogenic Disney dogs, cheerfully wagging their tails. The dead dog is the gift, the teacher, the messenger of God.

Imperfection is perfect. In Japan, fine tea bowls—usually made of the most delicate porcelain, exquisitely painted and glazed—are venerated as the embodiment of aesthetic and spiritual beauty. Treasured above all others is the Kizaemon Bowl. Ironically, the Kizaemon is a humble peasant's rice bowl, made clumsily by an anonymous Korean potter on a crooked wheel, unornamented, asymmetrical, smudged with sand and ashes, and veined with cracks. (The cracks recall our own cracked-and-treasured Liberty Bell, mythically linked to the declaration of our robust, rock 'n' rolling independence from the mincing, minuet-dancing symmetry of eighteenth-century Europe.)

Thus God asserts her loving presence in the very oddness of life. The enlightened, her true lovers, behold and embrace her in all that is odd, that is eccentric, that refuses to lace itself into the symmetrical straitjacket of rationality. In every act, in every breath, they live that unlaced freedom, whether as (say) a Tibetan crazy wisdom master who disrupts a formal temple service with a barrage of verbal abuse and flatulence, or as (say) an American hidden yogi who looks like any other Wall Street broker, whose body is laced into the gray suit and club tie but whose awareness dances naked with the Mother.

The unenlightened, failing to see the perfection of the imperfection of each present moment, keep waiting for the other shoe to drop, for that apocalyptic future when the supposed deficiencies and injuries of their lives are neatly paired up with supposed solutions; when they triumph over life's stubborn oddness; when they get even.

That moment will never come . . . thank God. (She loves me.)

• Many years ago a Buddhist woman named Sono taught this enlightenment practice, which is as powerful as it is challenging: throughout the day, no matter what happens, keep saying, "Thank you for everything. I have no complaint whatsoever."

• You can also heartfully invoke the Billy Joel Mantra: "I love you just the way you are."

Exploding Proverbs

✳

14. Seeing is believing

$\mathcal{S}$HOW ME.
    Belief arises naturally from direct experience. I believe zucchini plants grow from zucchini seeds because I've seen them do it. Why shouldn't spirituality happen the same way? Why should we be told we must turn this natural order of things around, that we can see God, or the Infinite, only by believing?

Certainly belief *can* give rise to the spiritual experience—anything can. We are so completely surrounded and pervaded by the Infinite that the wonder is not that anyone ever experiences it, but that *everyone* doesn't *always* experience it. In fact, there's nothing else to experience. All we need is the deep assurance that everything is okay, the permission to relax and let go into Existence just as it is, so that our clear perception of it may naturally dawn. For some people, belief in a kindly, loving deity engenders that relaxed assurance. Others, who find that being required to believe in a deity raises their blood pressure instead of lowering it, are wise to take some other approach.

Belief can also precipitate transcendental experience by blowing the circuits of the conceptual mind with a proposition that defies logic:

> *It is to be believed because it is absurd.*
> —Tertullian

Here the mechanics of belief superficially resemble those of the Zen koan ("What is the sound of one hand clapping?"; "Where does the wheel go when the hub is removed?"). The difference is that the koan is an absurd *question,* a catalyst that dissolves along with the mind it blows. Belief is an absurd *answer*—at the end of the process we're still stuck with it. If believing that God is a 200-foot-tall purple jellybean blows my mind into satori, that's cool. But now this big jellybean has taken over my living room and wants me to introduce it to all my friends. The transcendental experience gets mixed up with the *content* of the belief, whereas it's actually the *process* of believing that sparks it. We've confused the blownness of the mind with the particular paradox that happened to blow it. The side effect is a world full of conflicting beliefs, and believers who invest them with absolute importance: eventually we're at war over whether that jellybean is purple or yellow. Transcending through intense beliefs is like drinking cheap whisky—it'll get you high, but it can do a lot of collateral damage, much of it to other people.

So . . . show me. Give me the experience first, straight up. Don't bother asking if I believe in God (or Brahman, or nirvana). There's no right answer because it's the wrong question.

Belief has no more to do with the Infinite than it does with zucchini plants. Many seekers (sometimes under group pressure) contrive an attitude, a complex of emotions and ideas *about* the Infinite, and mistake it for direct experience *of* the Infinite. But the Infinite is what's left after all ideas and attitudes have been abandoned. To know God, to attain realization-liberation-salvation, you don't have to believe squat.

> *Curb your dogma.*
> —JERRY JARVIS

How, then, do spiritual systems sometimes come to demand belief? A dramatic example can be found in the early history of Christianity.* It arose, of course, from Judaism, the religion that venerates the supreme Yahweh, whose mysterious, unpronounceable name means "Essence-of-Being." (Most Bible translations render it "the LORD," thus, in one misleading syllable, portraying the Essence as humanoid, authoritarian, and male.) From Old Testament times onward, some Jews had always insisted that the radiant wonder of this Essence could be experienced directly:

> *O taste and see that Essence-of-Being is good.*
> —PSALM 34:8

Once such Jew, named Yeshua, whom we know by his Greek name, Jesus, seems to have been what Tibetan Buddhists call a

---

*Much of what follows is merely plausible speculation. Who knows what happened? *I* don't.

chigcharwa, an "all-at-oncer," someone so ready for realization that he needed only the slightest push to gain it instantaneously—apparently when John baptized him. Countless others had been dunked in the same river and had heard the same words, but Jesus got the juice. John's pronouncement that "The kingdom of heaven is at hand" seems to have acted for Jesus as a mahavakya, a "great utterance" that triggered an immediate, irreversible opening into transcendental Reality:

> *And, lo, the heavens were opened unto him, and he saw the Spirit of God descending like a dove, and lighting upon him.*
> —MATTHEW 3:16

At this time many Jews were looking forward to an external "kingdom of heaven" or "kingdom of God," a righteous political state in which Jewish law would replace Roman rule. Now Jesus declared that he could lead them to this kingdom, but he redefined it, in accord with his own experience, as an internal state of permanent communion with Yahweh, the boundless Essence that is always here now ("at hand"). Teaching with the great power that can come only from firsthand knowledge ("as one with authority, and not like the scribes"), he gathered students and sought to share his enlightenment.

But all-at-oncers are rare. The disciples, like most of us, were *rimgyipa,* "gradual-progressors," for whom the ripening of realization takes years of practice. The New Testament documents the frustration and escalating confrontation that arose from others' inability to "get it" all at once, as Jesus had. Finally, his execution cut short his teaching career after only one to three years (depending on which Gospel we read). Jesus was yanked off the stage just as he was clearing his throat—long before his disciples could attain or even clearly understand his state. (In the Gospels we see them repeatedly missing his drift.) Out of their mixture of confusion and passionate devotion, they now apparently shifted the definition of the kingdom a second time. Having failed to join Jesus in immediate boundlessness by transcending, they would join him in a future Paradise by believing and dying.

But *what* was one to believe? As we've seen, belief is most mind-blowingly effective when it defies logic. Certainly Jesus triumphed over death—like all the great masters, he experienced that we are not bodies that are born and die, but the changeless Vastness within which all changing appearances, including birth and death, take place. But in the emerging official doctrine, this sublime victory was reduced to the literal, antilogical reanimation of a corpse. Also, Jesus has been called "son of God," a Jewish term for anyone whose expansive nature resembles the Infinite as closely as a son resembles his father.

The morning star sang together, and all the sons of God shouted for joy.

—JOB 38:7

For as many as are led by the Spirit of God, they are the sons of God.
—ROMANS 8:14

But now the term gained a new meaning, and Jesus' beginning, like his end, was reduced to a prosaic miracle, perhaps borrowed from such popular pagan tales as Zeus' impregnations of mortal maidens. Belief in these twin miracles became the ticket to heaven, shifting attention away from what Jesus had taught by word and example: that the transcendental kingdom of God is always experientially at hand, here and now, open to all, beyond belief, no ticket required. Through his crystal-clarity of realization and poetic beauty of expression, he became an undying embodiment of that openness, in the form of omnidirectional, limitless love, which cannot be constrained by anything, least of all by what we think about him.

What do Taoists believe? What do Buddhists believe? Again, it's the wrong question. Westerners often assume that all religions are closed belief systems. But a religion can be an open experiential system. The Dalai Lama, for example, has said that if science contradicts the Buddhist scriptures, the scriptures will have to be changed. The Buddha himself declared:

> *Do not believe a thing because many repeat it. Do not accept a thing on the authority of one or another of the Sages of old, nor on the ground that a statement is found in the books . . . Believe nothing merely on the authority of your teachers or of the priests. After examination, believe that which you have tested for yourselves and found reasonable, which is in conformity with your well-being and that of others.*
>
> —KALAMA SUTRA

And now that the Buddha himself has joined the ranks of the "Sages of old," he will doubtless understand if we don't blindly accept things on *his* authority.

Does all this mean that faith plays no role in the growth of enlightenment? Not at all. But faith and belief are two different things. Faith is practical, a form of trust so basic to *everything* we do that we needn't think much about it. Just to drive down the road, with nothing to keep the oncoming cars from slamming into us but a painted yellow line, requires faith in the skill and sanity of our fellow drivers. In the same way, following a spiritual path naturally requires some faith in the teacher, the teachings, and ourselves—our ability to do the practices and evaluate their effects upon our lives. We're like novice mountain climbers: we need faith in our guide, in the knots he tells us to tie, and in our own ability to climb.

Faith is an instinctive wisdom that, like love (its other face), is deeper and broader than mere specific beliefs. Perhaps we grew up believing that Mom would always get us off to school in the morning, cook us supper in the evening, and have clean jammies waiting for us at bedtime. But even if not all the expectations on our little list were met, even if sometimes we had to pour our own Cheerios, we still loved her.

In other words, belief is conditional. Faith, in its highest form, is unconditional. It doesn't need to know that Jesus rose on the third day, or that Lord Rama rescued Sita from the demon Ravana, or that Nagarjuna retrieved The Tibetan Book of the Dead from the dragons under the sea. It is "the Peace of God, which passeth all understanding"—that is, it transcends all concepts. Just as willing suspension of disbelief helps readers leap into a story, willing suspension of conceptual belief helps us leap into nonconceptual Being. Faith allows me to truly let go, so that I don't care what I or anyone else does or doesn't believe. On the deep heart level which passeth all understanding, I can take God or Jesus or Padmasambhava or Existence for whatever they turn out to be, which is always going to be different from what I thought. I can let myself be surprised.

Rest assured: Any belief in which we rest assured will sooner or later be pulled out from under us. The trick is learning to rest *un*assured, to relax and dig the free-fall. Then anything can happen. Our experience in the very next moment may utterly overturn the experience of all previous moments. Maybe we'll wake up from this long dream. Maybe the illusion of separateness will fall away. Maybe the heavens will be opened unto us, and we will see the Spirit of God descending like a dove and lighting upon us.

15. Easy does it

*T*HIS PROVERB is more than folksy advice for deal-
ing with final exams and traffic jams: it's a universal
principle like $E=mc^2$, a succinct description of how things in
the cosmos work. And because meditation is a process for living
harmoniously in the cosmos, this same *de*scriptive law that governs everything from the motions of galaxies to the functions of
spleens is also the *pre*scriptive law that governs how to meditate.

At every moment, everywhere in the universe, the least possible work is being done. Lightning strikes along the path of
least resistance, and does it the first time, with no trial and error.
A drop of water falling in a vacuum is perfectly spherical,
spreading itself out as little as possible, tolerating as little surface
tension as necessary; when falling through air, it assumes a
teardrop form that is perfectly aerodynamic. A river flows between its banks because that expends less energy than overflowing, but the moment heavy rains make overflowing the easiest

thing to do, it overflows. The shapes of the continents, the size of a cloud, the design of our brains, the speed of the planets around the sun, the number of leaves on my sycamore tree and the exact order in which they fall in November: every feature of the universe represents the precise expression of this principle at work—or, rather, avoiding work.

As children resemble their parents, this most distinctive feature of the creation gives us a big hint about the "Creator." **Easy** (effortless, formless Being) **does** (spontaneously expresses itself as) **it** (any given form). **Easy** is the transcendental constant in the universal equation. **It** is the variable, for which we can substitute any phenomenon—photons, killer whales, April fluctuation in the yen. **Does** is the work that is not work, the doing that never loses the unruffledness of Being. God is the coolest of cool hands, the super-slick secret agent who foments each moment; who, no matter what's shakin', is not stirred.

So, to do anything "right" (in maximum harmony with the way of the universe) is to do it the easy, clean, streamlined, mathematically elegant way. But this principle is often misconstrued. The easy grace of unhurried efficiency is not the same as sloth. Thirty years ago, like many hippie mystics, I read the Tao Te Ching's declaration that "The way to do is to be" and twisted it to mean "Do nothing." In my zeal to do nothing full-time, I dropped out of college and all other productive activity. When I later dropped back in with a few years of meditation under my belt, I noticed that many of my old habits of dreading, evading, and needlessly prolonging my work had dropped away. I just did it. By my final semester I was taking two or three courses above the normal load and barely breaking a sweat.

Though he is moving easily, he overtakes them.
　　　　　　　　　　　　　　　—RIG VEDA

This easy grace is seen in the Taoist story of the butcher who uses the same cleaver for years without having to sharpen it, because he moves it through the spaces *between* the bones—the ox just falls apart. When Michael Jordan charges the net, he sees, in the clarity of an instant, the invisible space that winds through the defensive players; then he glides frictionlessly through that space; and the defense, like the ox, falls to pieces. Count Basie heard that same frictionless quality as the essence of jazz:

I think a band can really swing when it swings easy, when it just can play along like you are cutting butter.

And Van Gogh sought it in his paintings:

I envy the Japanese the extreme clearness which everything has in their work. It is never tedious, and never seems to be done too hurriedly. Their work is as simple as breathing, and they do a figure in a few sure strokes with the same ease as if it were as simple as buttoning your coat.

Now, if easy-doing it is the way to perform action, it should certainly be the way to meditate: just the opposite of the strenuous exertion people often associate with the word. There are many specific forms of meditation—the Malini Vijaya Tantra lists 112. In a sense, it's not what you do, it's the way you don't do it . . . it's the lack of strain with which you approach it.

There's a story about a disciple who asks his teacher, "O Master, how long will it take me to attain enlightenment?" The teacher peers at him, strokes his chin, and says, "You? Thirty years." Being an impatient Type-A, the disciple replies, "What if I give up my job and family, completely throw myself into it, and work as hard as I can?" "Then it will take sixty years."

Whatever form of meditative practice we adopt, sooner or later it becomes a process of non-doing, an act of letting go. So why not sooner? Since the whole point is to allow the mind to relax into the Vastness that we already are, working to control or concentrate the mind is self-defeating. A martial artist friend of mine once asked if I held the equivalent of a black belt in meditation. No black belt, I told him; no white belt, no green belt, no belt at all—pants fall down and there we are, in our original butt-nakedness.

The very word "meditation" is a stumbling block. It's one of those intimidating polysyllabic beauties, inherited from Latin, that make things sound complex and difficult. The Tibetans have a more graceful term, *gompa,* but they deconstruct even that one in the saying *Gompa ma yin, kompa yin*—"Meditation isn't; getting-used-to is." There's nothing to do; just get used to doing nothing. We don't attain enlightenment, we *are* enlightenment; just get used to the light. Since struggling will only entangle us in further complexity, to meditate we just be simple, just hang out and not-do, just allow the natural boundlessness of our essential nature to grow familiar.

I loaf and invite my soul.
—WALT WHITMAN

When we build a city we pour concrete and steel over the natural landscape, leveling the hills and superimposing a grid of streets and avenues upon them. But we leave an occasional pocket of space where we *don't* pour the city, which we call a "park." There's really no such "thing" as a park, just a space of not-city, but it's still a useful word—when we want to reconnect with the earth that underlies the city, we can say, "Let's go to the park." In the same way, the mind urbanizes the natural nakedness of boundless Reality, leveling its hills of unbearable beauty and pouring a grid of concepts and desires upon them. What we call "meditation" is merely a pocket of time in which we don't pour desires and concepts. There's really no such thing as meditation, just a time of not-grasping, but it's still a useful word—when we want to reconnect with our underlying luminous essence, we can say, "Let's meditate."

So, we just Be. We just relax our grasping, give up all our strategizing, and abide in innocent, childlike openness ("Unless you change and become like children, you will never enter the kingdom of heaven"); and, in time, the timeless nature of ordinary experience reveals itself by itself. We can't learn how to "do" it because there's nothing to do but rest in each moment's experience as it already is, continuing to be what we have always been: perfect, empty awareness, within which thoughts and sensations frictionlessly come and go.

That's all.

But . . .

That's very steep simplicity. It's supremely ironic that anyone should need training in non-doing. Most of us, though, with our ingrained habit of grasping, have to *learn* to just Be. This is why interaction with a teacher is important, why just reading a set of instructions isn't enough—or is *too* much. What we require is not really *in*structions but *de*structions, verbal and nonverbal cues (perhaps including such self-dissolving catalysts as visualizations, mantras, or koans) to soothe or startle us into letting go of the imaginary obstacles to abiding in what we already are. And we must abide *consciously*. Just as we need a walkway into the park so that we can *see* its wildness, we need the subtle skill of remaining vividly alert as we settle into Being.

The way of consciously communing with the simplicity of the Inexpressible is inexpressibly simple. Ultimately this non-process of non-happening is too intangible for anyone to teach; it can only be hinted at. But hints are everywhere, from The Tibetan Book of the Dead:

> *Rest in the pure, naked mind, luminosity-emptiness, which your guru has shown you.*

to the Beatles:

> *Let it be.*

From Thomas Merton:

> *Receive the light with passive and loving attention.*

to Andy Warhol:

> *The more you look at the same exact thing, the more the meaning goes away, and the better and emptier you feel.*

From Emily Dickinson:

I cling to nowhere till I fall,
The crash of nothing, yet of all.

to the Tropicana orange juice carton:

Nothing added—nothing taken away—not from concentrate.

From Yahweh in the Old Testament:

Be still and know that I am God.

to St. Paul in the New:

The day of the Lord [that is, the dawning of awareness of
Being-Essence] so cometh as a thief in the night.

We don't know when that thief will come; there's nothing
we can do to *make* him come (the more we bustle about, the
more our noise scares him away); but we can open all the doors
and sit quietly.

SUGGESTIONS FOR FURTHER PRACTICE:

• Again, it's best to receive meditation guidance from a live
teacher. But in case you're in some remote outpost, here's one
approach:
   Sit in a comfortable upright position with eyes closed and
hands loose in your lap or on your knees. Drop your shoul-
ders and relax. Take a slow, satisfyingly deep breath, totally
filling and emptying yourself; repeat a few times. Then allow
the breath to settle on its own . . . and just sit easily. . . .

Now, notice the natural sense of space within you . . . and allow the mind to rest there. . . . Whatever comes and goes within that inner spaciousness—thoughts, moods, sense impressions—let it come and go. . . . Don't focus, don't concentrate, don't manipulate, don't try to figure anything out. Simply rest, let go, allow, be. . . . When you find that you're clinging to some thought, fine—relax your grip and let go once more into the open space of inner awareness. . . . Again and again, let go into the openness. . . .

At some point, you might note whether that space has any particular shape or not . . . whether it has any boundaries or not . . . whether it's totally dark and flat, or there's some subtle sense of aliveness, of luminosity. . . . Whatever's there, just rest aware. . . .

• If you feel the need for something more substantial to rest the mind upon, you can use your breath, or a sound (a bell or gong fading into silence, the delicate mental echo of a mantra), or one of the body's inner energy centers (heart area, lower belly). Easy does it—simply keep relaxing into the object of meditation and letting everything else go. If the object seems to be melting away, let go of it as well. You can also start with any of the other practices described in this book (prayer, chanting, guru yoga, tonglen), then just sit and be. Pedal for a while, then coast.

• At the end of a session, you might want to take a moment to mentally share the benefits of your practice with all other beings who desire the same happiness and liberation that you do. Then open your eyes slowly and ease back into activity.

16. Practice makes perfect

HEN CHARLIE "BIRD" PARKER, the high-altitude saint of the alto saxophone, was a teenager in Kansas City, he used to drive his neighbors crazy by practicing scales for sixteen hours a day. Through that rigid discipline, he was preparing to become the co-inventor of bebop, one of the most radically fluid art forms ever devised. Only when he had the scales literally at his fingertips could Bird improvise his intricate melodic lines, with their incredibly complex, high-speed shifts from key to key. Only then could he use notes that were wildly "out" (harmonically unconnected to the original tune); he knew the structure of the "in" notes so thoroughly that he could hear precisely how far and in what direction the out notes were out, even when improvising at a hundred miles an hour. Before you can blow as free as a Bird, you have to practice, to get your chops down. In the same way, before we attain the infinite freedom of enlightenment, most of us will have to log many thousands of hours of meditative practice. **Practice makes perfect.**

Or, as Bird himself said, "First, learn your instrument. Then forget about all that—and just play." "Play" is a telling word here. Playing is what children do. Jesus, who says we must be like children to enter the kingdom of heaven, also says, "Be ye therefore perfect, even as your Father which is in heaven is perfect." Children play perfectly; they improvise with the innocent, "heavenly" spontaneity in which whatever happens is just right. For the jazz musician this means to leave off judging each note—just play it in the moment, hear its inherent perfect rightness, and hear how it implies the next perfect note that wants to flow from it. Likewise painters and their brush strokes, poets and their words. We practice craft till we can forget about craft and create in the state of unconditional openness, where we literally love each note, stroke, or word. This love is the amazing gracefulness where nothing we do is a mistake, where whatever we do is effortlessly perfect.

> *Love is the fulfilling of the law.*
> —ROMANS 13:10

This perfection is not perfectionism; it fulfills, the easy way, what the perfectionist seeks the hard way. My mother, God bless her, was a language perfectionist. She used to go to the local Taco Bell and, carefully rolling her Spanish R's, order a "bur-r-r-r-r-r-rito." Unfazed by smirking clerks, she knew she was winning points in language-maven heaven. But there are no points for being right, for being perfect in the perfectionist sense. There's no one keeping score but ourselves.

Perfectionism correctly intuits that there must be some kind of perfect, all-redeeming state of life. But it fails to recognize that the perfected state is always *already* attained. We don't have to change anything, fix anything, clean anything; we just have to open our awareness wide enough, relax into our original child-like playfulness deep enough, to see it. Spiritual practice reveals that *this* world is perfect, that we need no heaven of perfectly coifed and neutered angels, no utopia of perfectly pronounced fast foods. Thus practitioners in the Dzogchen, or "Natural Great Perfection," tradition, considered the highest teaching of Vajrayana Buddhism, meditate with their eyes (and all their senses) wide open, fully accepting each moment of experience just as it is.

But realizing that perfect state takes practice. We have to set our buttocks on the chair and do it—not just when our fickle intellect approves, or when we feel sufficiently "spiritual" (or desperate), but day in and day out, like brushing our teeth.

Eighty percent of success is showing up.
                              —WOODY ALLEN

I'm an amateur saxophonist. Sometimes I practice with the big book of Bird solos, his spontaneous flights transcribed by some painstaking musicologist. I can read the notes, first slow then faster, trying by osmosis to absorb some of Bird's bebopping freedom. Parker never parks, so the Bird in the book is not the living, breathing, unreadable Bird in the moment. But it is a Bird in the hand.

No time to practice? Nonsense. No matter how busy we are, we may get a phone call and talk for five minutes or fifteen, and we still somehow take care of all our busy-ness. As spiritual practitioners, we get a call from God every day. *Never* put God on hold. No *place* to practice? Nonsense. We can practice anywhere. We don't need our favorite meditation cushion, we don't need silence, we don't need incense, we don't need nothin'. I love the serene privacy of my bedroom or my garden, but I've meditated in parks, churches, doctors' waiting rooms, planes, trains, automobiles, buses, bus terminals, a broom closet, the lee rail of a sloop underway to Santa Catalina Island, the back of a motorcycle bumping over the Sierra Nevada mountains, and (one time) the unused ladies' room of a porn theater in San Francisco.

It's important not to be dissuaded, especially in the beginning, by the unevenness of experience. Meditation is a knack that gets familiar with practice, a sort of unused muscle that has to be developed, like wiggling your ears. More accurately, everything else that we do (forming coherent sentences, being "selves") is an elaborate set of ear-wigglings which we've been practicing most of our lives. Meditation is simply the letting go of all such wigglings and resting in what's left . . . which is even more effortless than Bird wiggling his fingers on the saxophone keys.

But if it's so simple, why do we need to practice at all? This is the Paradox of Practice. There's really no practice to do, but to realize that, we have to sit in our seat not-doing it. It's important not to be confused when teachers say there's "nothing to achieve": those same teachers have spent years practicing and perfecting their nonachievement. Lama Surya Das, the American-born Dzogchen master, captures this paradox when he says, "Practice *is* perfect." We do put in hours and years of practice, but not in the spirit of trudging laboriously toward some distant goal; we rest weightlessly in the Natural Great Perfection of each moment; we practice long and easy.

The Buddha formulated this idea of perfect practice in his Fourth Noble Truth: *marga,* path. The way to extinguish suffering, he said, is to practice the Noble Eightfold Path: perfect view, perfect resolve, perfect speech, perfect conduct, perfect livelihood, perfect effort, perfect mindfulness, perfect meditation. On one level, these are prescriptive guidelines for living— perfect speech is both truthful and uplifting, perfect livelihood is the work that most benefits our own well-being and the world's.

But if we take "perfect" in the perfectionist sense, the Eightfold Path is a recipe for neurosis. Rather, the Buddha invites us to enjoy, like children at play, the natural perfection inherent in all areas of our lives. There's nothing absolute about the number eight—we could also analyze our lives into four areas or a hundred. The point is that practice doesn't end on the meditation cushion (or in the church, temple, or dojo). All the mundane dreck we have to wade through between practice sessions *is* our practice. To get the maximum number of minutes for morning meditation, I used to rush through my shower before and my commute after. But hurry-up-and-relax doesn't work; it's *all* meditation, and if I can't have Great Emptiness in the shower and Great Compassion in New Jersey traffic, I can't have them on the cushion.

There's a story in Chinese martial-arts tradition about a young man who begs a great Kung-fu master to teach him the Iron Shirt exercises, an esoteric system reputed to make the muscles and organs so strong that they are impervious to blows.

The master at first refuses, but finally sets him a *kung* (a formidable challenge). Pointing to a thick tree, he says, "Pull up that tree and bring it to me; then I'll teach you Iron Shirt." After months of futile tugging, the student notices that he can get better leverage if he keeps his back straight. With further experimentation he finds the optimal way to plant his feet. He works on, incrementally adjusting the way he hugs the tree, the way he breathes, the way he visualizes the task. After four years the tree starts to give. Finally he uproots it and lays it at the master's feet, demanding, "Now teach me Iron Shirt!" "Now I don't have to," the master replies. "You've just learned it."

So, on the path of practice, we have to go through whatever we have to go through—each step of experience is part of what we're learning as well as the necessary prelude to the next step. (This is another sense in which practice is perfect.) Here the greatest inspiration to diligence is the example of the masters, but only if we see them not as superpersons but as ordinary practitioners who made it. When we're sitting in meditation, our busy mind churning and grinding, and we're ready to call it quits, we can ask ourselves, "Did Gautama, on his way to becoming the Buddha, ever have a meditation like this?" When we're limping to the dojo with a torn knee, wondering why we should bother, we can ask, "Did Morihei Ueshiba, on his way to becoming O'Sensei, ever struggle with physical injuries?" When that insufferable person confronts us with unforgivable behavior for the hundredth time and we are tempted to harden our heart against him, we can ask, "Did Jesus, on his way to becoming the Christ, ever have to forgive the unforgivable?"

These exemplars remind us that what we're finally perfecting is ourselves, that practice makes *us* perfect. That is what's attainable. What else are you doing with your life?

SUGGESTIONS FOR FURTHER PRACTICE:

- Many people find it useful to commit themselves to a minimum amount of practice every day, no matter what, whether thirty minutes, ten, or even one. The days when we "can't meditate" because of personal pressures or increased responsibilities are exactly when we most need to plug into the silence. It's also helpful to have a set time for practice— say, after the morning shower, during the coffee break, before supper—so that we don't keep intending to "get around to it" and then find the day is over. Just sit.

- Sometimes emergencies seem to arise almost conspiratorially to dissuade us from practicing. These are actually creations of our own mind. Ironically, the mind feels at home with its familiar limitations and, when they are threatened, rebels by creating illusory crises. This struggle is represented in the paintings of St. Anthony praying and fasting in the desert, resolutely ignoring the devils that assail him; and of Lord Buddha meditating beneath the bodhi tree, visited by Mara's seductive and terrifying visions, all intent on derailing his vow to practice till enlightenment. Whether we're beset by seductive demons (Mmmmm, Häagen Dazs! Eat! Now!) or terrifying demons (Yeeeowww, deadline! Rewrite! Now!), the key is to be steadfast. Just sit.

• Meditation means facing our essential perfection, but it also means facing our fear, boredom, anger, and doubt. On our way to crystal-clear vision of the Changeless, we'll be put through whatever changes are necessary. We may find ourselves crying, laughing, shivering, sweating, fidgeting, shaking. Sometimes we may feel like snoozing, sometimes like jumping up and tearing the furniture apart. It's all part of the ride—and, as with a roller coaster, it's advisable to remain seated till the ride is over. Just sit.

17. An apple for the teacher

A IS FOR Apple, Apple is A—the beginning of knowledge, the beginning of the alphabet, the first day of school. A is also *Ahhh!,* the end of knowledge, its culmination in epiphany, in satori, in orgasmic release, in the explosion of constricted conceptualization into endless Awareness-Space.

Apple falls in the fall. Apple is our fall from grace, from the Garden of naked Being. We give this apple to the teacher—we offer up our confusion to the master, the guru, the lama. She can handle it; she devours it.

Apple is a wholesome, simple, straightforward fruit. **An apple for the teacher** is the correct way to approach the guru: with wholesome intention, simple gratitude, straightforward honesty. Good apples and good students are crisp—they're sweet but they bite back a little.

Apple is the offering, the fruit given in *puja,* the rite of thanksgiving to the guru: we give back to the teacher the fruit of her teaching, the fruit of expanded awareness as the bounty of life. Others see us making offerings and bowing and they think we're doing something for the teacher, but it's all for us. Such rituals open us to receive, align us to make our connection. (As the sign in the gas station reads, "TANK MUST FACE PUMP.") At first this thanksgiving may feel contrived. But as we come to realize the value of the teaching, spontaneous gratitude grows into genuine devotion. Someone once asked one of my teachers why he bowed down before a picture of *his* teacher. He said, "I don't bow down, I *fall* down."

The miracle of the teacher, almost more than his grasp of enlightenment, is his grasp of ignorance. From the point of view of realization, ignorance is impossible, incomprehensible, devoid of all reality. "And he marveled because of their unbelief": Jesus is bewildered that everyone doesn't get it. Can't they *see* that the kingdom is at hand—here, now, inside us, all around us? So we offer the teacher these flowers, these apples, our service, these feeble gestures to keep him connected to the world of ignorance, where we need his interaction:

> *People think I'm crazy for enjoying things like placing his* zori *[sandals] just right so that when he steps off the mat his feet hit them exactly in stride. You put them one place rather than another because you know your teacher's stride. All of this is part of the immersion, the purification, the service, the totality of the experience.*
>
> —RICK STICKLES, AIKIDO-SENSEI

I am Infinity that has forgotten itself. The teacher is Infinity that has, to at least some degree, remembered itself—yet, because she is fully human, she can help me remember too. Being human, the teacher has a personality, and personalities are different. Some teachers eat yogurt and vegetables, some eat steak and whisky. Some live in caves, some live in condos. Some have formal status as lamas or rabbis, yogis or priests, some don't. Some are crude, some are refined, some liberal, some conservative, some flamboyant, some reserved, some gentle, some fierce.

A disciple of Avatar Meher Baba, who was considered an incarnation of the Divine, once remarked his surprise that Baba was clean-shaven: "Does God stand before the mirror and shave every morning?" Baba replied, "I am more human than you can ever be." What did Jesus blow his nose on? What did the Buddha think about when he walked off from the crowd to take a piss? If such images offend us as irreverent, we're reverently splitting divinity from humanity, precisely missing the point these divinely human teachers teach.

I'm always wary of any alleged holy person who flunks the Funny Voice Test—who uses an affected, dramatic voice when he talks about God. To realized people, the Sacred is the most natural thing in the world, the very warp and woof of every-moment experience. If they had to use a funny voice to address it, they'd have chronic sore throats. One of my students, surprised at a master's casual humor in a taped lecture, said, "I thought enlightened people would have this . . . *air* about them." Well, no: a master is one who has *cleared* the air. We've all seen too many stone Buddhas, too many solemn Bible movies full of actors acting illuminated, carrying their ersatz enlightenment like some fragile jar balanced precariously on their heads, nursing their saintliness like a bad case of constipation. They miss the joy, the ease, the matter-of-factness of realization, which is too subtle for the flash of cinematic drama.

Out of amusement and compassion, the master plays with his humanity, and so takes the pressure off the rest of us, undercutting our aspirations to be constipated saints and RoboBuddhas. I know one lama who blows a mean blues harp, one who's an avid *Star Trek* fan, one who loves Cuban cigars, and a few who fret aloud about losing their hair. I once sat at lunch in a New York restaurant with a noted spiritual teacher. He listened politely as I grappled aloud with some tangled spiritual problem I thought I had. Suddenly he interrupted me: "Wait a minute—this is important." I awaited the revelation, the flash of wisdom that would dispel my darkness. "The waitresses in this place are really incredible." I looked around. He was right; they were gorgeous. And the simple, relaxed, human awareness that notices and gratefully appreciates such here-and-now blessings was exactly what I, in all my labored introspection, had missed.

So we offer the apple of our life to the teacher. He may bite into it with great delight, or slice it and dice it, or pitch it back at our crotch (Neem Karoli Baba actually used to do this), or grind it into applesauce and dribble it down his chin, or plop it on our head and aim his crossbow at it, with steady or unsteady hand. This ungovernability is the teacher's job. The teacher confronts us with inexplicable events and insoluble predicaments. He tells us to stand up and sit down at the same time. He's completely unreasonable—he's there precisely to upset the applecart of our reason, to introduce the element of radical disorderliness every time we think we've got things in apple-pie order.

The teacher is always coming from out of left field, from the wild corners of awareness our logic has excluded. She's like the adult in a "Peanuts" cartoon, half in and half out of the frame, speaking to us kids in a mysterious, buzzy language. We want her to give us what we want, but she keeps giving us what we need. (She's guaranteed to disappoint.) We want her to play the role of the guru as we've scripted it, but she shreds our scripts as fast as we can write them. Finally it's just her and us on an empty stage, unrehearsed and scriptless. (She's the one that's not terrified.) The drama that transpires necessarily involves confusion, tension, and occasional resolution—from our side. From her side, she's just hanging out and Being.

To annoy us out of our habitual patterns, to induce us to break out of self-imposed limitations, a skillful teacher pushes our buttons. Like a mischievous child on an elevator, he'll punch *all* the buttons of our personality and force us to see what's on every floor. As I handed one of my teachers an early manuscript of this book, he said, straight-faced, "Oh, maybe there's some good material here I can steal." *That* put me through some changes—one simple comment gave me a good look at thirty-one flavors of paranoia, pride, guilt, confusion . . .

Because the Infinite is bigger than any one personality, it makes sense to learn from more than one teacher. As a lama explained it to me, this is like having two eyes: it gives us depth perception, so that we do less bumping into things. Still, the time may come when you're ready for the intense dynamics of a committed relationship with one teacher. But entering into such a spiritual marriage without considerable maturity and self-knowledge can be disastrous. The spiritual highway, like the divorce courts, is strewn with the wreckage of unions made too young, too lightly, or for the wrong reasons. And, as in marriage, some suitors that look promising turn out to be frauds, loonies, abusers, or just not Mr. Right. The Dalai Lama suggests that before committing to a teacher you "spy" on him for several years. A true teacher breathes eternity, *is* eternity, and will always be there—there's no hurry or pressure.

Neither does the true teacher flaunt whatever realization she may have attained. The statement "I am enlightened" is never true: for the unenlightened there's no "enlightened," and for the enlightened there's no "I." (Actually, for the enlightened there's no "enlightened" either—there's just Reality.) Since enlightenment is the transcendence of conceptuality, there's no way to evaluate another's enlightenment conceptually. So committing to a teacher on the basis of his presumed enlightenment is a shaky enterprise. It's enough (it's plenty) that a teacher competently dispenses authentic spiritual knowledge and practice, that he has integrity, and that you feel somewhat resonant—at home—with him.

Relating to teachers is tricky in any case because of the way we project onto them. It is said that the student creates the teacher: we conjure true teachers out of our genuine spiritual aspiration, and false teachers out of our desire to magnify our neuroses to cosmic dimensions. Slavishly groveling before a teacher that one has exalted as the Best and Only is a sneaky form of egotism—*I'm* groveling before the *best!* Once, at the end of a lecture, a group of us stood as the guru was leaving the platform. On his way down, he stumbled for a moment on the steps. After he left the hall, an argument broke out over whether he had really stumbled, with several fervent disciples staunchly maintaining that he could not have, because perfect masters don't make mistakes.

If we demand teachers who are superhuman caricatures of realization, who never stumble, never hurt, never cry, we mis-define realization and so block ourselves from experiencing our own innate realization in this moment. The teacher is nobody special. In fact, he's nobody at all, just boundless openness; that's why he can help you realize that you are too. And that makes him the most special person in the world. Even if it were within the teacher's power to manifest as an outwardly flawless, ideal being, she probably wouldn't do it. That would just encourage us to fixate on her as one more false absolute, instead of raising our gaze to the level of the one real Absolute. Jesus repeatedly (and unsuccessfully) attempts to deflect such fixation:

> *Why do you call me good? There is none good but One—that is, God.*

Any such unbalanced view of the teacher tends eventually to swing the other way: when we realize he's not the plaster Christ we tried to make him, we feel betrayed and denounce him as anti-Christ. We're good at this—in politics and show business as well as spirituality, this setting up and tearing down of icons is as American as apple pie.

The relationship with the teacher, like most spiritual prac-tices, works over time. There may be crucial, dramatic moments of direct transmission. But being consistently, undramati-cally connected with the teacher and the truth he embodies, day after day, is what eventually heals the diseases of ignorance and suffering. An apple for the teacher a day keeps the doctor away.

We may connect with a teacher we've met only through books or pictures, whose body may be distant in space or time. We may connect with what is called the Inner Guru, but even this term may be too limiting. There's ultimately only one Teacher, of whom "outer" as well as "inner" teachers are manifestations. Tibetans call this the Vajra Guru—the Diamond Teacher, who, like a diamond, is brilliant, clear, indestructible, precious. Not only all flesh-and-blood teachers but all phenomena are regarded as agents of the Vajra Guru. When everything we behold is our Teacher, everything that befalls us is his teaching: every smile of a child or crick in our neck is the Teacher's pointing to our own nature, to the boundless nature of all things. Then everyone and everything is our guru, and apple trees of wisdom blossom everywhere.

SUGGESTIONS FOR FURTHER PRACTICE:

- Our time here is limited, and so is the teacher's. The way to draw the best teaching out of the teacher is not to make some extravagant display of melodramatic devotion but simply to show you won't waste her time. Show up, suit up, ask your questions, and *listen* to the answers—don't be so busy thinking up clever objections that all you hear is the rattling of your own intellect.

He that hath ears to hear, let him hear.
                                        —MATTHEW 11:15

• *Guru yoga,* or meditation on the form of the teacher as a gateway into the Formless, is a potent spiritual technique. (In a sense, Christianity is an elaborate system of guru yoga, with Christ as the guru—or the Blessed Virgin, for those more attuned to the feminine aspect of the Infinite.) Select a picture of your teacher or of anyone who embodies vast openness in a form with which you feel some resonance. Then easily rest your gaze on the picture. The teacher, by virtue of having realized her own formless omnipresence, is literally present in the picture. She's also everywhere else, and so are we, but through her form she opens the *experience* of that reality to us.

• In another variation of this practice we dispense with the picture. With eyes open or closed, just relax, feel the presence of the teacher all around you, and rest your awareness in that. In the initial stage there may be some visual sense of the teacher's outward appearance, but after some time let that dissolve, leaving only the teacher's inner essence. Let it run through you, wash over you, inside and out. Completely open to it; melt into it. Then, after a while, let even *that* dissolve, leaving . . .

18. Speak of the Devil

Speak of the Devil and he's bound to appear.

✳

H E IS INDEED. The Devil is a rumor, a product of speech that has gained a powerful cumulative reality in the lives of millions of speakers. But the Devil is just an extreme, dramatic example. *Whatever* we speak of appears.

The named is the mother of all things.
—TAO TE CHING

Studies have shown that the more names we have to distinguish subtle shades of colors, the more shades we actually see. All of our experience is shaded by the names we speak: Are those freedom fighters or terrorists? Is she a courtesan or a whore? Is he pro-life or anti-choice? Is this a rerun or an encore performance? Are you eating leg of lamb or the leg of a lamb? I'll have my attorney call your shyster.

Such names can give others power over us. One day in the fifth grade I learned that what I had been blithely calling a fly was "really" a *Musca domestica*. In that moment I surrendered power to those high priests the scientists, who knew the "real" names that I would never learn for dogs, trees, rocks. It didn't occur to me that those long Latin names were no more real than the homely Anglo-Saxon ones.

But enough speaking of speaking. Let's speak of the Devil. Most cultures don't have a Prince of Darkness, a singular embodiment of absolute evil, one-stop shopping for the terrors of the soul. Why does the West find it necessary to invent him? Our unique need for Satan arises from our ambivalent feelings about God. The Vast One, the Formless, the Infinite, can never be limited to a finite form. *God blows your mind*—that's God's job. The experience of God is nirvana, the "blown away" state. (The unpronounceable divine name Yahweh, spelled YHWH in Hebrew, may be an imitation of a gust of breath—perhaps even an amazed "Whew!") So, like Moses and his descendant, the transcendental poet Jesus, we celebrate the effulgent Emptiness, which is enshrined in the radiantly vacant inner sanctum of the Temple and in the sanctum between our own temples.

But also, like the serious Caesars who seized Jesus' legacy, we resist the anarchic implications of having our minds blown. We want God to be a big Guy, a beefy, benevolent despot made in the Emperor's grave image, graven throughout the empire and (indelibly, unblowably) in our own minds. But once we isolate a good, order-imposing God by skimming him out of the continuum of boundless Existence, our sense of symmetry requires that we also isolate an evil, chaos-wreaking anti-God. The divine Emperor is so heavy, we need an equally heavy anti-Emperor to sit at the other end of our universe. Then we can cast them as mortal enemies, locked in an apocalyptic game of seesaw to the death, with our soul (whatever that is) as the prize.

And now we have drama! In movie houses and churches alike, the Prince of Darkness is the number-one ticket seller. We reward this superstar with his own kingdom, a parody of the heavenly one, so that we can give ourselves a jolly scare contemplating an eternity of baroque punishments for such crimes as having the wrong thoughts light our minds or the wrong sensations warm our loins. It's all so much more entertaining than the simple gospel of love and forgiveness, of a kingdom of God whose door is always wide open. The good news that the kingdom is within us means we can never be cut off from God. Jesus saves us by making us see there's nothing to be saved from. Like all the great masters, he's a spiritual grown-up who sets our hearts at peace by lifting the covers and showing us there's no monster under the bed, and so helps us become grown-ups ourselves. But there's something so cozy, so familiar about remaining children . . . so we keep bringing the monster back.

The Devil is the animated shadow of our hidden fear. He is the embodiment of all the parts of ourselves we have denied, come back to haunt us; he is the slime monster that rises from the clogged cesspool of our psyches. And this cosmic boogeyman is backed by troops of irredeemable dupes. Thanks to the Devil, we can gather up all our unnamable free-floating dread and give it a name: Nigger, Whitey, Faggot, A-rab, Kike. Just as a finite God saves us from the blinding, mind-blowing light of nirvana, these finite devils save us from the creepy-crawly terrors of the night. Satan and his agents put the darkness into a form we can strike at. Speak of them with the right name, and they appear as devilish, nonhuman beasts, deserving of slaughter. Cops round up not suspects but "mutts"; demonstrators clash not with police but with "pigs." In our various wars we have killed not people but "Jerries," "Krauts," "Japs," "Slopes."

So then. If we're the ones who have made the Devil appear, we should be able to make him vanish by applying the Buddha's Third Noble Truth ("Don' do like dot!"). Here are some approaches we might adopt.

SUGGESTIONS FOR FURTHER PRACTICE:

• Explore the relativity of names. Repeat a word till it's rendered meaningless, till you experience it like a foreigner hearing it for the first time. (Your own name is an interesting place to start.)

• Listen to your use of negative, judgmental language. Don't necessarily try to stop. But listen honestly. Also note such expressions as "I hate you" or "I'm gonna kill you," which, even made in jest, affect the consciousness of both speaker and hearer. "God damn it" is a particularly interesting expression: By calling upon God to damn something, we are structuring a dualistic world where individual things (and people) are separate from the Sacred and can incur its permanent, infinite wrath. Then we have to live there.

• Listen as well to your tone and subtext. Sarcasm can be a particularly insidious, destructive mode of speech. If you think teasing your kids is funny, think again.

• Most important, stop feeding the Devil by stuffing stuff into your psychological junk drawer. *Repression feeds obsession.* Mere thoughts, no matter how horrible—even the most alarming murderous scenarios or incestuous fantasies—can't send you to hell. The fire of hell is right now, ignited by the friction of attraction and repulsion when "bad" thoughts are repressed. But obviously, acting out such thoughts would lead both us and our victims to be dragged through a far messier hell. Instead, just calmly *experience* the thoughts, without the usual anxious alternation between indulgent pulling toward them and guilty pushing away. Both pulling and pushing only knot us up more tightly. As we let the thoughts simply be, they untangle naturally. Breathe, relax, and allow them, in their own time, to dissolve into the natural Vastness of the mind's own nature.

Here we may take a lesson from Padmasambhava, the great Lotus-Born Guru. His adventures in the course of bringing the enlightenment teachings to the wilds of Tibet can be read (on one level) as archetypal events within our own expanding awareness. Padmasambhava's exploits include subduing countless indigenous spirits—embodiments of the mind's wildest impulses—and transforming them into guardians of Dharma. Confronting them all in one grand showdown, he sings:

Within the empty mandala of mind essence,
Appearance and existence, gods and demons, are easily accommodated.
They are accommodated, yet still there is vastness.

Within the empty mind essence, beyond concepts,
Neither gods nor demons exist.

Whichever magical trickery you display before me,
I am not moved even the slightest.
There is no way you can destroy the nature of mind.

As long as we abide in the luminously open nature of mind, none of our illusory devils can have power over us.

19. Beauty is in the
eye of the beholder

AITING FOR my bags at two in the morning in the Palma de Mallorca airport, and eager to try out my high-school Spanish, I strike up a friendly conversation with three idle baggage handlers who are passing around a bottle of red wine. After a few minutes, one of them motions toward the group of Americans I'm traveling with. "*¿Porqué son tantas feas las americanas?* (Why are American girls so ugly?)" I reply, "*No, no es verdad. ¿Porqué lo dice?* (No, it's not true. Why do you say that?)" In a universal male gesture, he cups his hands in front of his chest. "*¡Las españolas dan una mano completa!* (Spanish girls give you a real handful!)"

Okay, so Spanish men like 'em hefty. Value judgments are subjective. **Beauty is in the eye of the beholder.** Greta Garbo has no inherent quality of beauty, the Elephant Man no inherent quality of ugliness; the aesthetic distinction is one hundred percent our own projection. That's astonishing enough, but within this proverb lurks an even more astonishing revelation. When we behold the apparent perfection of Garbo's face, or of the *andante* movement of Beethoven's Seventh, or of Michael Jordan's turnaround fade jump shot, we're looking into a mirror. That face, that sound, that shot is merely reflecting back to us the innate perfection (the **Beauty**) of the awareness (**the eye**) that **behold**s it.

James Joyce approaches this understanding in *A Portrait of the Artist as a Young Man* when he describes the experience of beauty. The mind, he says, is charmed by the harmonious proportions of a beautiful object and settles into a "luminous silent stasis." In this moment the mind feels complete, as it apprehends "the clear radiance of the esthetic image." What Joyce doesn't quite say is that this "radiance" of the object and the "luminous" quality of the mind are one and the same—the Clear Light, or Ground Luminosity, which is the very nature of existence and awareness. The object, by momentarily lulling the mind out of its usual restless seeking, catalyzes its settling down into its own overlooked, blissfully silent nature.

Art makes nothing happen.
        —W. H. Auden

The *Ahhh!* of luminous aesthetic stasis is essentially identical to the *Ahhh!* of luminous meditative stasis, satori. And because, especially in the West, satori has been so widely neglected in formal spiritual practice, this blissful epiphany has moved from the temple to the opera house, the movie house, and the basketball court.

Historically, as our religions became more doctrinal and less experiential, we Westerners sought transcendence in the fine arts; they became our substitute religion, stirring the kind of passion the church once inspired. But now, when few doctors and lawyers, let alone carpenters and bricklayers, read sonnets for pleasure as they did in Keats's day, the most popular gods of the sacraments of aesthetic bliss are athletes and movie actors. In centuries past, we honored our gods by elevating them into constellations. Now we acknowledge their celestial radiance by calling them "stars" and paying them astronomical salaries.

People who say they're not interested in "spiritual" experience, then, just don't recognize that they're relishing it regularly. When Jordan levitates skyward with three defensive players on him, hangs in the air for an impossibly long moment, adjusts his spin, adjusts his look, makes the swish through the waving forest of arms and heads, then draws the foul on the way down— not only is the play perfect, *everything*'s perfect. For that moment our awareness is completely focused on the perfection of the act, recognizing in it a reflection of its own perfection; nothing else exists. This is a true meditative state.

Meditative *practice* simply means learning how to experience isolated moments of this everything-perfect state independently, without an aesthetic object to reflect it; and then learning to prolong those moments and integrate them into our lives. Through meditation and devotion we grow to see the clear radiance in *every* face, every sound, every movement. The arc of the wino's glowing cigarette butt flicked into the gutter is as breathtakingly graceful as Michael's finest shot. We thank the extraordinary beauty of art, sport, meditation for initially opening our eyes, then behold the ordinary beauty that is everywhere.

This, perhaps, is why Jesus scolds those who seek miraculous happenings or "signs." Such a frame of mind divides existence into the miraculous and the mundane—it keeps us from seeing that the mundane is indivisibly miraculous. If we wait for the sun to stand still, we won't see the miracle of its motion; if we wait for people to walk on water, we won't see the miracle of their swimming (or sinking). Everything is exactly the way it is, and that couldn't be more astounding.

> *The kingdom of heaven is spread upon the earth, and men do not see it.*
>
> —THE GOSPEL ACCORDING TO THOMAS

My daughter taught me a lot about this way of seeing when she was a baby. One winter afternoon I watched as, fascinated, she examined the wood grain in the back of a chair illuminated by the brilliant sunlight that streamed through the window. Through her eyes I saw how unspeakably rich that simple experience was . . . and, by extension, how much of that richness I usually filtered out as "irrelevant." This is yet another sense in which we must be like children to enter into the kingdom—to take off the blinders of jaded adult perception.

This is the "Sabbath Mind" of Jewish mysticism, the state of awareness in which God stepped back from his handiwork and "behold, it was very good." When, beyond doing and judging, we can rest and just be—first momentarily, then permanently—we see, as God does, that it's all unutterably beautiful. Thus resting in the Sabbath is the central practice for maintaining the Covenant, the intimate relationship with the Infinite. When Jesus advises, "If your right eye offends you, pluck it out," he is inviting us to let go of judgment. (The right eye is connected to the left cerebral hemisphere, and hence to the analytic, discriminative mode of perception.) He also says, "If your eye is sound, your whole body will be filled with light." When we open up and allow ourselves to behold the perfect beauty that surrounds us at every moment—not only when hiking through the Maine woods at sunset, but when driving through the Holland Tunnel at rush hour—our lives are filled with light, ease, joy.

Once, when my wife was vacationing in Rome, she hired a tour guide for a day, looking forward to his sophisticated explication of the city's artistic and architectural sights. But as it turned out, he knew little English and less art. All he could do was point to one masterpiece after another and say, "See how it's-a nice!" As we grow in awareness and sense what Buddhists call the "one taste" that runs through all perceptions, we still perceive distinctions—we still see the difference between Michelangelo and *merde*. But at the same time we open to it all and we see how it's-a nice.

SUGGESTIONS FOR FURTHER PRACTICE:

- Cultivate your appreciation of beauty wherever you've overlooked it. If you think bowling is dull, watch a bowling match and appreciate the grace of a perfectly rolled strike, the energy and concentration of the competitors. Listen to a style of music you normally dislike and hear what its devotees hear in it. In the country, open your eyes to the beauty of the starry night; in the city, see the beauty of the smokestacks.

• When you see someone you would normally consider ugly, intuitively grope toward the way Buddha or Rembrandt would see him. Would the actual physical features be different? What *would* be different? Then delicately feel your way toward seeing (and hearing, smelling, etc.) *everything* that way.

20. It's better to give
than to receive

*Y*EAH, SURE. Tell us another one. Give us some more transparent Sunday school propaganda, some more clumsy attempts to bamboozle us into voluntarily renouncing our voracious hungers, into swallowing back the saliva of our insatiable drooling for more—more possessions, more stimulation, more of whatever we can get more of. At least give it to us straight. Tell us it's *necessary* to give if we're going to coexist civilly rather than destroy one another in a violent chaos of competing appetites. Tell us it's *wise* for the haves to placate the have-nots with occasional scraps of charity from their tables. But don't tell us it's *better.*

It's better.

It's not better in the context of the reality model that most people maintain, in which we are finite, limited beings, separate from one another and from the universe. If that's our model it makes perfect sense to grab as much as we can get away with.

In fact, if that's our model it's probably better to be true to it, to grab boldly and see where that takes us, rather than dilute the experiment with grudging gestures of altruism we've been shamed into pretending to feel. If the values we serve clash with the reality in which we think we live, we're committing metaphysical violence, even as we're giving physical comfort to the orphans and widows. If I'm really just an isolated self zipped into a bag of skin, then I should cram as much good stuff as I can into the bag. Receiving, then, is the highest, the only ethic; giving is a delusion born of sentimentality, sloppy thinking, or fear. Mother Teresa was a fool, Gandhi was a dupe, the robber barons were at least philosophically honest.

But then why do such bald-faced declarations of selfishness cause us such revulsion? And why have we all had small or large experiences of "the joy of giving"? Why, as we grow more mature, do we find that the best part of Christmas is not opening our presents but watching our kids open theirs? Are these not hints of a deeply held intuition that the self-in-a-bag model is flawed? Again, if we're merely separate waves on the ocean of Existence, we may as well gather as much water as we can, plundering it from other waves if necessary, before we crash against the shore and vanish forever. But if we look rigorously at our supposed separateness—if we search for the dotted line that separates the wave from the ocean, and thus from other waves—we see that there is no line. You are the ocean.

Thou art That.
—CHANDOGYA UPANISHAD

From this radical shift of view follows a correspondingly radical shift in values. Giving (and all such ethical behavior) affirms our oceanic status, reminds us of our forgotten nonseparateness from the "other" to whom we give. To treat another unkindly, in this model, makes as little sense as punching oneself in the nose. That's why giving gives us joy: it frees us from the cramped illusion of separateness and gives us a glimpse of our vast, non-separate nature.

> *A human being is part of the whole called by us "universe," a part limited in time and space. He experiences himself, his thoughts, and feelings as something separated from the rest—a kind of optical delusion. This delusion is a kind of prison for us, restricting us to our personal desires and to affection for a few persons nearest to us. Our task must be to free ourselves from this prison by widening our circle of compassion to embrace all living creatures and the whole of nature in its beauty.*
>
> —ALBERT EINSTEIN

When we acknowledge the futility of trying to gain fulfillment by stuffing ourselves full, we free ourselves to do just the opposite, to abide in the empty bliss of simply Being. And we confirm and enliven that experience by giving to those "others" whom we must compassionately embrace as part of ourselves in order to *have* the wholeness of our Being.

Does this mean we have to take a vow of poverty to gain realization? Probably not. Can I keep my computer and my Coltrane CD's? Probably. If spirituality were inversely proportional to affluence, Skid Row would be teeming with saints. One can be just as attached to a loincloth and begging bowl as to a Mercedes and a closetful of Armani. It's not so much what you have as whether you define yourself by it, and thus how tightly you grip it.

Renunciation is not giving up the things of this world; it is accepting that they go away.

—SHUNRYU SUZUKI-ROSHI

True, some people are so caught up in the clutter of possessions (the pride of owning, the worry of getting and keeping) that the shortest path to freedom may be to dump them all, as in the case of the young man whom Jesus advises to give all his wealth to the poor. (We're never told what happens to him after he walks away, "grieving, for he had many possessions." Does he eventually take the plunge? If not, is he able to enjoy his possessions as he did before, knowing the spiritual price he has paid for them?) But clutter and clarity alike are ultimately states of awareness, regardless of how much stuff we may have.

For that matter, giving does not have to be about stuff. The source of this proverb is Jesus, whom St. Paul quotes in the context of explaining "that so laboring ye ought to support the weak." Service is often the gift that most lightens others' burdens while it enlightens our own minds. Hinduism calls this way of altruistic action *karma yoga* and recognizes it as a genuine mystical path. Perhaps the most familiar form of karma yoga is parenthood. When we get up at two A.M. to feed the baby, we find out that it's okay to miss some sleep; when we work a second job to put our kid through college, we find out that that's okay too. If we were an isolated wave, it wouldn't be okay. And if we can extend this impulse of selfless service beyond the nearby waves of our immediate loved ones to include all waves, we affirm our oceanhood powerfully. The very word "selflessness" has two meanings—altruism and enlightenment—which turn out to be equivalent.

Unselfishness is no different than that non-dual openness, vast emptiness, Shunyata.
—N Y O S H U L   K H E N P O   R I N P O C H E

This virtue is literally its own reward; vice is its own punishment. The kingdom of heaven is within you; so is the kingdom of hell. Heaven is awareness enjoying its own blissfully expansive nature. Hell is awareness tied up in knots, strangling itself in the illusion of constriction. Giving and the other virtues, being expansive, reveal our awareness to be heavenly. Selfishness and the other vices, being constrictive, make it feel hellish. As we grow into enlightenment, spontaneous virtue becomes natural, vice becomes naturally unthinkable. We can work it from both ends: being good gets us to heaven, and being in heaven makes us good. As finite, unfulfilled selves in a stumble-bum search for fulfillment, we did bad, selfish things. As we realize we're infinitely fulfilled not-selves, selfishness ceases to arise.

This is the true joy in life . . . being a force of nature instead of a feverish selfish little clod of ailments and grievances complaining that the world will not devote itself to making you happy.
—G E O R G E   B E R N A R D   S H A W

The Lene Lenape Indians say that long ago the Crow had beautiful, rainbow-colored feathers, sweet-flavored flesh, and a melodious voice. One day it began to snow. The snow kept falling until it was burying everyone on earth. Rainbow Crow volunteered to fly up and ask the Great Spirit to make the snow stop. The Great Spirit answered that he could not so violate the ways of nature, but he gave the Crow fire to melt the snow. As

Rainbow Crow flew back toward earth with the fire stick in his beak, it singed his rainbow feathers to a sooty black, roasted his sweet flesh to a smoky taste, and choked his melodious voice till it was harsh. He saved the people, but then began to weep for his lost beauty. Just then the Great Spirit appeared to Rainbow Crow. He told him that indeed his beauty was lost, but that in exchange he had gained freedom: no one would ever hunt a bird with sooty feathers, smoky flesh, and a harsh, croaking voice. And if he looked closely enough, he could still see rainbow colors in his feathers—reflected from the world he had saved.

The soaring freedom and the rainbow resplendence with which this tale ends point to the state we attain by serving and giving; they hint at its being a state of spiritual exaltation. In fact, in the original wording of this proverb, Jesus says, "It is more *blessed* to give than to receive." This blessedness is the realized state, in which (like this savior) we save ourselves from being petty consumers and narcissistic preeners, endlessly reinforcing our smallness by trying to stuff ourselves bigger. Giving, like devotion, meditation, or any other spiritual practice, turns out to be a matter of letting go.

SUGGESTIONS FOR FURTHER PRACTICE:

- One way to give is simply to bless people. Christian practice is particularly strong in its emphasis on praying for others in all circumstances. The Tibetans have a powerful technique, called *tonglen,* literally "giving and receiving," in which we mentally exchange our happiness for the unhappiness of others. Visualizing any fellow being or group, with each inbreath we take in their pain and confusion in the form of hot, greasy, foul-smelling smoke; and with each outbreath we give them the cool, clear, healing light of our own happiness. By directly challenging our deeply held habit of keeping all pain "out there" beyond our bag of skin and accumulating joy "in here," tonglen cuts through the false duality of out and in, freeing us further into the state of blessedness.

Ironically, tonglen frees you from fixation on your own suffering. In the decades since the invasion of Tibet by the Chinese Communists, many Buddhist monks and nuns have endured prolonged torture by doing tonglen on behalf of their torturers.

• Giving should be as anonymous as possible. Otherwise it can become just another form of getting—getting gratitude, getting approval—in short, a means of reinforcing our small-waveness instead of letting go into the ocean, which Jesus calls "the Father."

But when you give alms, do not let your left hand know what your right hand is doing, so that your alms may be done in secret; and your Father who sees in secret will reward you.
                                                    —MATTHEW 6:3–4

• Every moment is a chance and a challenge to give; forget "I gave at the office." If nothing else, we can give our simple presence, our openness, our right-now Being. The air around some people feels like a spring day—the plumber who whistles cheerfully while fixing your faucet, the nice old lady who chats with you on the bus, neither of whom may have spent a minute in formal spiritual practice. They project a spaciousness in which we naturally relax, a sense that everything is somehow okay. When the masters share this presence with others, it's called *darshan*. As we grow in consciousness we're giving some measure of darshan to everyone we meet.

21. To err is human,
to forgive divine

*O*NE OTHER important form of giving is *forgiving.* The paradox is that the way to attain flawless, enlightened, **divine** awareness is **to forgive**—to allow everyone **To err**, to be flawed, ordinary, **human**s, including ourselves. Of course, everyone's going to be flawed whether or not we "let" them; if we defer our loving acceptance till they become flawless enough to suit us, we'll have to defer it forever. Forgiveness connects us to the inconceivable level where not only we but all the imperfect, erring others are perfectly divine.

Forgiving is not forgetting—it doesn't require us to be stupid. It's only sensible to avoid the block where we've been mugged and to get the mugger locked up where he can't harm others. But we need not carry within us a big, carefully tended lump of toxic blame labeled "MUGGER," which only poisons us and blinds us to the perpetual openness of life in which others may grow and redeem themselves.

The dynamics of blame are all too familiar. Another driver cuts me off or pokes along, blithely blocking the passing lane. My muttered response ("Asshole!") affects my own consciousness more than his, since he can't hear me. As I finally pass him, I make sure to get a good look at his face—I want to *see* that asshole. And, sure enough, assholism is painted all over him, plain as day. Of course he's really just another flawed, divine human like me, but through blame I have clouded my own vision too much to see that. To forgive is to relinquish blame and so reclaim the clarity of our vision.

For that matter, if I regard all my circumstances as the display of the Diamond Teacher, as my own boundlessness shaking off the particular structures of ignorance in which I have encased it, then there is nothing to forgive; whatever befalls me is precisely the pointing-out of Reality I require. Another way to say this is that everything is our own doing and our own unfolding, the educational ripening of karma we planted in the near or distant past. This attitude is not "blaming the victim"; it's giving up the principle of blame altogether. The Dalai Lama works ceaselessly for the liberation of his homeland, but by regarding Mao Tsetung and the Communist Chinese forces that have ravaged Tibet as his greatest teachers, he has shown that even victims of a holocaust need not perpetuate the cycle of blame into future generations. They can make the buck stop with them; they can forgive and remember.

Confronting this issue is crucial for real spiritual growth—just meditating and waiting for our attitude to become more charitable is not enough. It's true, in principle, that to realize enlightenment we need only relax into omnipresent Vastness. But the subtle tensions generated by blame and resentment keep us from fully relaxing. We may have brief glimpses of satori, but without profound forgiveness these tensions will keep pulling us out. Meditation is surrender to the present moment; our surrender can't be total if inside we're fighting the wars of the past.

I once had a vivid experience of this truth while on a retreat. One day, after several hours of meditation, I was feeling very comfortably ensconced at the hub of things; great clarity and wholeness of Being seemed to be radiating in all directions. Suddenly I noticed an obstruction—a tiny dark spot in one corner, where my awareness felt somehow stuck. As I focused on it, I realized it was a former lover, someone with whom I had had an unhappy breakup many years earlier. I realized that I had been carrying feelings of betrayal, abandonment, and resentment ever since, and that those feelings had been distorting all my relationships, blocking the clear, omnidirectional flow of awareness and love. The only way to melt that blockage was to forgive. As I forgave her from the deepest depths I could reach, intense, wrenching emotions began to pour out of me.

After some time, I felt that I had made my peace with her. But now the faces of others for whom I had been carrying buried resentment began to present themselves. I continued meditating, forgiving, purifying, as I saw before me in turn each person who had ever injured or betrayed me: lovers, teachers, family members, every school-yard bully who beat me up as a kid, the two thugs who mugged me as an adult. Then I saw those who had filled me with fear from a distance: dictators, torturers, killers. The final challenge, the Minotaur at the center of my dark Labyrinth, was Hitler—evil incarnate. After considerable struggle I found that somehow I could forgive even him.

But there was more. After I felt that I had forgiven the whole world, my own face appeared before me, and I saw that I constituted a whole other world to forgive: moral failings, personality flaws, even body parts that had betrayed me with their weakness. Finally, after several hours of this, exhausted but purified, I felt able for the first time to fully love myself as well as all other beings. I felt as if a great rock had been rolled off my heart, as if deadly poison had been leached out of all my tissues.

I wish I could say that this one dramatic experience permanently elevated me into a state of all-loving sainthood, but it doesn't seem to work that way, at least in my case. Such tidy resolutions happen only in the movies. I've muttered curses at several pokey drivers since then, and worse. So forgiveness is an ongoing process, and while it's going on I can at least forgive myself for not being a saint. But eventually, I'm convinced, it *can* become a perpetual state, a permanent junking of the blame mechanism. To *forgive* literally means to "give beforehand"; true forgiveness is a blanket absolution of everyone for all possible errors, past, present, or future—a clean slate in each new moment.

> *Then Peter came up and asked him, "Lord, how often am I to forgive my brother if he goes on wronging me? As many as seven times?"*
>
> *Jesus replied, "I do not say seven times; I say seventy times seven."*
>
> —Matthew 18:21–22

The immediate beneficiary of this gift is ourselves. We break free from our tangled web of past hurts and recriminations (waking from our personal nightmare of history) and our exaggerated anxieties about the future ("Perfect love casteth out fear"). We are born again into an immaculate world of clarity and light by baptizing others in the pure waters of our forgiveness, fresh moment after fresh moment.

SUGGESTIONS FOR FURTHER PRACTICE:

• A good time to practice forgiveness is at the end of a meditation session, or after you've hiked into the woods or done any other activity that makes your awareness feel settled and expansive. Focus on someone for whom you have been harboring resentment—whoever pops into mind. Notice that this resentment is not a mere abstract notion but an almost palpable entity or energy, perhaps in your chest or abdomen or suffused throughout your blood or bones. Now, either mentally or aloud, tell the person you forgive him, and as you do so let that physical feeling of resentment evaporate through all your pores. If other feelings come up in the process, ride them out. Keep expressing your forgiveness and releasing the resentment till you feel clear, or till you feel you've had enough for one session. Always finish by forgiving yourself.

• You can also do a similar practice of apologizing to those you've injured. Interestingly enough, they're often the same people you feel have injured you.

• Gradually integrate the practice of forgiveness into daily life, silently releasing others from blame as you interact with them. Note that this does not mean simpleminded passivity: that's as much a cop-out as angry reactivity. The really interesting challenge is to forgive people internally even when appropriate action demands that, externally, we deal harshly with them.

• If you prefer the gutsball approach, from this moment forward just forgive everyone for everything.

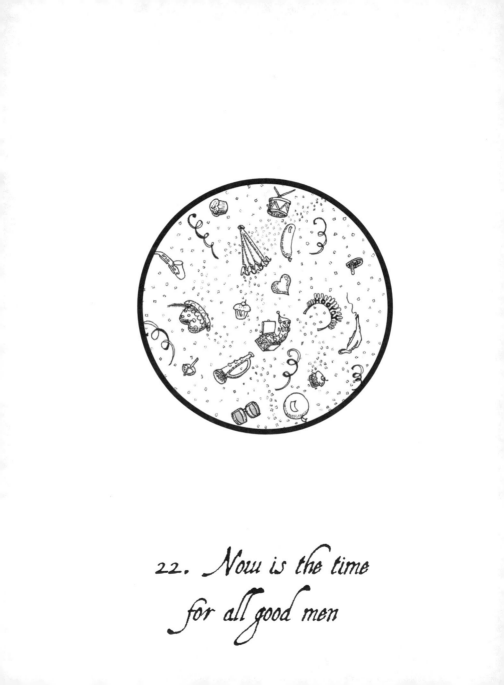

22. *Now is the time for all good men*

Now is the time for all good men
to come to the aid of the party.

✳

IN 1867 a court reporter named Charles Weller composed this sentence to test his friend Christopher Sholes's newfangled typing machine. Ever since, people trying out typewriters have used Weller's jingle. But it's actually a terrible test sentence; it leaves out almost a third of the alphabet. Why, then, has it persisted? What is the hidden appeal, the deeper truth, the covert message we feel compelled to type to ourselves?

Certainly there is that rousing call to take immediate action. As we've seen, there's no time like the present because there's no time *but* the present. *Carpe diem,* naturally—what is there to seize *but* the day? We can stew in our good intentions forever, or we can realize that **Now is the time**. But exactly who is our **party,** and why **come to the aid**? A party is a group united by a common interest. We're interested in liberation, which requires realizing the illusory nature of separate selves; thus our party includes all beings, from whom we're nonseparate. Our family, neighborhood, nation, planet, universe—all await our decisive, selfless action.

In the Bhagavad Gita, Lord Krishna, the embodiment of the Infinite, transmits his supreme teaching not to a member of the priestly brahmin caste but to a man of action, Arjuna the warrior. In fact, it's on a battlefield that he teaches Arjuna *Yogastah kuru karmani*: Established in union with the Eternal, engage in action. Once we're established in the timeless now, it's always time to come to the aid. Enlightenment is not passive bliss; it's timelessly liberated awareness, taking timely action to aid and liberate those who suffer in time.

It's now or never. If we truly realize that now is the time, even seizing the day is not enough. A day is too chunky a unit, seizing too crass an act. We need to let go in the moment—and let go *of* the moment. If it's never the past or the future, how can there be even this synapse between past and future that we call a moment?

Now-aware is the naked, unadorned wisdom-body of enlightenment.

—H.H. DUDJOM RINPOCHE

In fact, the more closely we examine our customary picture of time (some vague notion of moments lined up like beads on a string), the more suspect it looks. If we try to perceive one moment—where it begins, where it ends—we see that even a moment is too chunky a unit. Time is not chunks, not particles, not things at all; the word "moments," being a noun, merely disguises them as things. Behind the disguise lurks an impossible, paradoxical, strange-but-true kind of time, in which the world turns and people are born and die, yet it's always now. This is now-*and*-never time, the timeless time, the ever-fresh time in which everything, like Moses' bush, is ever burning but never consumed.

Toothless sages smile smiles of toothless babies
In Now-Now, Never-Never Land, where
Peter dances in the emptiness (the nick)
Of time, laughing
At Captain Hook, who's hooked
On visions of future conquest, haunted
By clock-ticking croc of future death.

We may catch this drift just by hanging around long enough. As we age, our sense that time moves faster, that it becomes less substantial, is a wearing-thin of the fabric of time-illusion. The more our future passes into past, the more clearly we see we have only the present. Our first reaction may be panic: *Wait—I just got here—I'm too young to get old.* But if we can relax into it (even as our hair and memory vanish as magically as they appeared), this anguish of mortality is prelude to the exaltation of eternity.

So then, if now is indeed the time, Weller's typing exercise may hint at another kind of **party.** What are we waiting for? Why segment our consciousness in time, working glumly from Monday to Friday, waiting to squeeze into a roomful of people on Saturday night, call it a "party," and work at being happy? *Now* is the time to party. Break out the noisemakers and the funny hats! Exude ease and joy in *this* moment, in *this* crowd, celebrating not only our own goodness (as Jack Horner has taught us), but everyone's. They're all **good men** and women, so invite them all. Our celebration of every moment must include every person and thing, every inch of experience.

Paradise is where I am.
—VOLTAIRE

Every night is prom night.
Everyone's your prom date.
—GIDEON LEWIS-KRAUS

The time is now, the party is awareness, the men and women are good, we come to their aid by inviting them all. This is the actualization of the Bodhisattva Vow to bring all beings to realization; the Vow is not (only) some heavy responsibility to be fulfilled over aeons—it's (also) the joyous enlightening of all beings by now-including them in our now-enlightenment.

This is the advice that Horwitz the cabbie obliquely offers in Salinger's *The Catcher in the Rye.* Holden Caulfield, seeking escape from his cold world, asks a symbolically freighted question: Where do the Central Park ducks go when the pond freezes over? Horwitz, knowing that the answer is not to fly away, not to duck, shifts the subject to fish:

They live right in *the goddam ice . . . Their bodies take in nutrition and all, right through the goddam seaweed and crap that's in the ice. They got their* pores *open the whole time. That's their* nature, *for Chrissake.*

This response contains the entire practice in a nutshell. We stay "right *in* the goddam ice"—in the moment as it is, in the world as it is, nonjudgmentally, no matter how ice-coldly it seems to treat us, opening our awareness-pores 360 degrees to the perfection-nutrition that's always present in the "crap." That's our Christ-like *nature,* for Chrissake.

After all, what's the alternative? Seeking perfection, the kingdom of heaven, is the blessing and curse of being human. If we don't find it now, we crave it elsewhen, and then we lose the present, which is all there is; we miss the party. Kicking this habit takes some serious non-doing. The plot curves of movies and novels, the crescendos and climaxes of symphonies and sex—all conspire to keep us hooked on some future moment as the place of resolution and fulfillment. But reminders of the perpetually nonculminating nature of absolute Reality are everywhere—even on the back of the dollar bill, where the uncompleted pyramid of time and works is completed by the eye of now-awareness. The fat lady never sings; her silence is deafening.

My favorite Jewish folk-mantra is *Nu?* Delivered with a rising, half-ironic inflection and a palms-up shrug, it means "So?" or "Well?" But its literal meaning is "Now?" In that sense it's a mindfulness exercise, anchoring us in the ever-present present. Our traditional affliction, however, our self-inflicted stress, comes from incessantly asking the question and never answering it. "Now," indeed—*what* now? The answer is, Relax now, let go into the now, and let natural perfection be. The Messiah (the manifestation of the Eternal One in time) is neither lurking in some prophetic future nor enshrined in some scriptural past; she is now-here or she is no-where.

The Buddha is the present moment.
—LAMA SURYA DAS

All moments are equally full; there are no "big" moments. If we're planning for joy later, we'll have it never—then we're like Disneyland tourists, deadening ourselves to the hours spent standing in line, waiting for the brief thrill of whooshing down the Matterhorn. All time is quality time if we're awake. If we're asleep it's all dead, no matter what we spend trying to hype and jazz it up.

Once when I was little, I heard a bantering quiz-show host ask a contestant, "What was the happiest day of your life?" The question haunted me. What would *I* say? Now I know the answer: Today. What happened today? Nothing special.

How long does it take to get enlightened? One moment—*this* moment. We're enlightened the moment we penetrate the moment.

SUGGESTIONS FOR FURTHER PRACTICE:

• Whatever's happening, this is it—rest in that. (What else can we do?)

• Never wait, always be.

• Never hurry either. This doesn't mean we can't move fast. But while moving, be vividly aware of the totality of experience in each moment. We usually blur moments together by ignoring "small," "unimportant" ones. Instead, choose to un-blur them by seeing (and hearing, feeling, tasting, smelling) everything. For example, I'm getting up in the morning to go to work . . . Hold it: Getting up in the morning includes getting out of bed, walking down the hallway, washing up in the bathroom, eating breakfast . . . Hold it: Washing up in the bathroom includes brushing my teeth, showering, shaving . . . Hold it: Shaving includes taking my razor . . . Hold it: First I grasp the left edge of the mirrored medicine cabinet door with my left hand, swing it open, catch it in mid-swing with my right hand, reach my left hand toward the second shelf . . . Hold it: As the mirrored door swings open, my reflected face swings past—whiskery cheeks, puffy eyes, tousled hair, white shower curtain behind me, a tiny fleck of dried toothpaste spittle in the lower corner of the mirror. Through the window on my right comes morning light and hoarse croaking of an agitated crow. The tile floor is cool beneath my feet . . .

The point is not to slow down our actions, but to open up our awareness. We can smell the roses without stopping. As we slice the moments smaller and smaller (refining those illusory particles ever closer to annihilation), they become fuller and fuller—like the galaxies-within-galaxies of fractal patterns, or the final seconds of a close NBA playoff game, where there's more and more action in less and less time. *Guarantee*: If you practice this exercise diligently you will never be bored, and you will develop the sensitive alertness of a basketball player, artist, or poet.

• On seizing the day: When I start getting lazy and distracted from my priorities, I sometimes fantasize a sort of cartoon version of what might happen five minutes after I die. I'm standing at some variation of the Pearly Gates, where St. Peter or Lord Yama asks me, "Well? Nu? Did you liberate yourself and others? Did you write your books? Did you laugh with your children and dance with your wife?" I'm reduced to replying, "Well, no, but I saw this really interesting infomercial about these miracle knives . . ."

• Notice how the mind contracts from its natural ease when a "problem" arises. Then relax out of that contraction. When, for example, you get a big piece of stringy celery stuck between two back teeth, there's a tendency to fixate on it; relaxed awareness of present perfection gets lost in present tension and anticipation of future relief. When you get the celery out at last, completely enjoy the *Ahhh!* of release—but note that, if we don't fixate, that *Ahhh!* is actually available in every moment.

• If you're sexually active, your letting-go-in-the-moment meditation will naturally include sex. Let go totally, experience totally, not only at the moment of orgasm but in *every* moment of lovemaking. Ironically, for all the urgency with which people invest sex, most don't really experience it once they're having it; they're too busy anticipating the near-future moment of orgasm. Notice how the body tenses up in that anticipation. Again and again release that tension and that future, and relax into what's happening right now. Together in timelessness, you and your partner will have a much better time. You can't hurry love.

• Just be present in the presence of whatever presents itself in the present. It's all a present.

Accidental
Hymns

✳

23. *Home on the range*

Oh, give me a home where the buffalo roam
And the deer and the antelope play,
Where seldom is heard a discouraging word
And the skies are not cloudy all day.

Home, home on the range,
Where the deer and the antelope play,
Where seldom is heard a discouraging word
And the skies are not cloudy all day.

✳

*O*H, GIVE ME A HOME: The trouble with words
like "enlightenment" or "realization" is that they make it
sound like something foreign or exotic, something special or extra. But it's not something extra that we add to life; it's something fundamental that we merely stop overlooking.

The aspects of things that are most important for us are hidden be-
cause of their simplicity and familiarity.
                                    —LUDWIG WITTGENSTEIN

Enlightenment turns out to be the simplest, most familiar of all
possible states. It is in *un*enlightenment that we are strangers in a
strange land. Enlightenment is just coming home or, rather,
noticing that we only dreamed we left. Home is where the heart
(the core, the essence) is. Home is our beginning and end; after
running the bases, it's where we come in safe.

We anticipated this homecoming back in third grade, when we sang this song so lustily, shouting out our prolonged, exuberant **Home, home**, unwittingly chanting *Om, Om,* the sound that represents infinite completeness, the home of all existence. We unwittingly reveled in Om's somatic completeness as well, with *ahh-ooh-mmm* resonating sequentially in our chest, throat, and skull.

What is the nature of this home of which we sing? **The range** is the open space where cattle graze, unhampered by fences. Assuming the first-person role of the cowboy (**Oh, give me**), we request and celebrate vast, fenceless freedom, which is the nature of that signified by Om. All Western movie aficionados know that fences are erected by farmers, the natural enemies of cowboys. To farm is to be earthbound, invested in cautiously calculated cycles of planting and harvesting. The farmer (the movie farmer of our imagination) is timid, henpecked; he lives in a house with a wife, unlike the macho-monk cowboy who roves the range in a womanless brotherhood, free of karmic entanglements, disdaining to plant his seed in ground or womb.

The farmer, then, is the aspect of our lives and minds that is caught up in the dimensions of time (the relentless seasons) and space (fenced-off land), cause (seed) and effect (crop). While the farmer pushes the plow in rigid straight lines within carefully surveyed squares, getting his bread by the sweat of his brow, the cinematic cowboy has aimless fun, riding his horse in non-Euclidean meanderings through an Edenic realm, where bounty for his cattle sprouts, free and uncultivated, out of the ground. He sows not, neither does he reap, nor gather into barns. This vision of the anarchic cowboy as the ideal form of absolute freedom is immeasurably appealing. We all wanted to be cowboys when we grew up; who wanted to be a farmer?

But how can we be at **home** on the range, on this empty Vastness where no home stands? To be home on the range is to rest where there is no resting place, or, as the Prajñaparamita Sutra advises, to "abide in abodelessness." Until we resolve this koan, we're apt to get tangled in frustration as our minds struggle and fail to locate boundlessness. The breakthrough comes when we realize that we can't locate it because all locations exist *within* that boundlessness, as does the struggle, as does the mind. We're like fish that have been swimming about, searching for the water.

Jesus' description of this abodeless state—"Foxes have holes, and birds of the air have nests, but the Son of Man has nowhere to lay his head"—is often mistaken for a lament, a declaration of noble sacrifice. But it's really a declaration of independence. As in the Appalachian hymn that exults "I ain't got no home in this world anymore," Jesus here celebrates his state of liberation. His cowboy wanderings with his apostle pardners in tow is a brilliant teaching not of an on-the-road lifestyle, but of an on-the-range mindstyle.

We see the same sense of utter freedom in Jesus' gestures of anarchy, such as defending the violation of the Sabbath (a demarcation of time) to pluck grain from a field (an act of timeless, cowboylike grazing, probably accomplished by hopping over some farmer's fence). The Bhagavad Gita says:

> To the enlightened brahmin all the Vedas [the complex regulations
> of orthodox life] are of no more use than is a small well in a place
> flooded with water on every side.

When our cup runneth over with enlightenment, all the orthodox rules and regs have served their purpose. As we transcend the illusory constrictions of time and space, we transcend the constrictive codes that govern time-space-bound behavior. ("The Son of Man is lord also of the Sabbath.")

And all we do to make our cup run over is get used to (become at home on) this open range of boundlessness where we've always been. Because "Meditation isn't, getting used to is" (Gompa ma yin, kompa yin), it's just a matter of being in the openness of Being, learning to let the mind rest with no visible means of support, or rather acknowledging that its usual supports (judgments and concepts, time and space, attraction and aversion) are fences of illusion. We don't have to tear down the fences. Just as we are always naked under our clothes, mind is always naked under its concepts—which is why it clings to them so stubbornly. But by loosening our grip on that fig leaf, we get used to our natural Edenic nakedness of mind.

So, heeding Jesus' warning, we build our home on the range not on the shifting sands, but on the rock. Paradoxically (again . . . always), what is most dependably rocklike is the transcendent, which is entirely insubstantial. What appears most substantial (the world of things) turns out to be just a procession of shifting, relative concepts passing through our awareness.

> *Form is emptiness, emptiness is form.*
> —HEART SUTRA

Farmers form farms by cutting up the emptiness of the range into parcels. The mind forms things by cutting up the emptiness of pure Being into parcels. This is the process of *reification* (literally "thingification"). Children on their first airplane ride are often shocked not to see a purple California and a yellow Nevada, as on the schoolroom map. All "things" turn out to be pretty much like that—conceptual conveniences, good enough for navigating on the ground, but less convincing when seen from a higher view. (Is your face a thing? Or is it a conceptual assemblage of several things, such as eye, ear, mouth? Or is it millions of atom things? Or a fraction of an organism thing, or an infinitesimal fraction of a species thing, or . . .)

Cosmic cowboys live a life as formless as the range on which they dwell. This they do by **roam**ing and **play**ing like the wild, undomesticated animals they encounter there. Those **buffalo, deer**, and **antelope** reflect precisely the three qualities of the qualityless transcendent as described in the Upanishads:

- The massive **buffalo** is an apt symbol for implacable *sat* (rhymes with "what"), absolute Existence, reality so emphatically real that, like Jesus' rock, it can never be diminished in time or space. All time-and-space-bound "things" abide within it and are nothing but it; all beings be in Being.

- The nimble **antelope** corresponds to *chit,* Awareness. The transcendent is not dead, flat, inert, but lively, vibrant, awake. Chit is the very awareness within which this sentence resonates right now, which is boundless. (Quick—where are its boundaries?) Everything happens within "our" awareness, but it is not ours in a limited, fenced-in sense in which we are somehow the proprietor of awareness. One moment of clear attention reveals that there is no proprietor, that the things we thought we were (name, body, thoughts, feelings, personal history) are merely impressions experienced within the unfenceable, unownable Awareness that we actually are.

• The gentle **deer** embodies the sweetness of *ananda,* Bliss— happiness beyond happiness. The changing, limited forms of happiness, whose opposite is sadness, are pale reflections, incomplete glimpses, of that Bliss which is our own true nature. It has no opposite: nothing can oppose it because nothing is outside it. Hence Jesus could say that when we look within we find heaven, that it is like a pearl of great price, to buy which we will gladly sell all else—all lesser forms of happiness.

Challenged to name the greatest commandment of the Hebrew law, Jesus says, "Thou shalt love Yahweh thy God with all thy heart, and with all thy soul, and with all thy mind." In Hindu cowboy lingo we might say, "You will fully commune with the open range of your own boundlessness, imbibing the ananda of deer, the sat of buffalo, and the chit of antelope."

The Dzogchen teachings outline three steps of realization: *direct recognition, not remaining in doubt,* and *continuing in the state.* Up to this point, the song has promoted the *direct recognition* of our own Vastness, our home on the range. Now, the line **Where seldom is heard a discouraging word** introduces the second step, *not remaining in doubt.* When words of doubt and discouragement come from others or from our own unsteady minds, we must grapple with them but not fixate on them. Gradually, with increasingly solid experience of unsolid Existence, the habit of doubt falls away of its own. As we get used to the freedom of no-self, we realize there's no one to be discouraged and no one to discourage them.

Similarly, **the skies are not cloudy all day.** The sky above the enlightened cowboy's head is also open, as cloudless as the range beneath his feet is fenceless. While we're still in the process of gaining realization, the skylike nature of our awareness is sometimes clouded; limited states of waking and sleeping, elation and depression, constriction and expansion reflect imperfectly the full value of the Limitless. But as long as the skies are not cloudy *all* day, as long as we get an occasional glimpse of clear blue, we're reminded that the sky rolls on and on, even when we don't see it. That's enough to keep us going.

One night, on a meditation retreat in the Oregon mountains, I was walking with Ram Dass under a gloriously star-studded sky. I sighed, "Ah, stars! These are not available back home in central New Jersey." He replied, "Well, actually they are. *You're* not." In the third step of realization, *continuing in the state,* we're cloudlessly, smoglessly available to that sky of Vastness in all its glory, all the time.

24. $\left(I~can't~get~no\right)$
Satisfaction

'Cause I try and I try and I try and I try . . .
—Words and music by
Mick Jagger and Keith Richards

✳

ONCE, IN HIS old age, Groucho Marx was asked by an interviewer what he would change if he had his life to live over. He replied, "Try more positions." This is funny, like almost everything Groucho said, but it also captures succinctly our failure to gain fulfillment—**satisfaction**—despite the widening variety and escalating intensity of our finite experiences. As the finite keeps refusing to satisfy us, we keep turning it to different positions, finding different angles from which to enter or be entered by it, but, as they say in Yiddish, *Gornisht helfen*—"Nothing helps."

It has been said that we are all born with a God-shaped hole in our soul and spend our lives trying to fill it with other things.

My soul thirsteth for thee, my flesh longeth for thee in a dry and thirsty land, where no water is.

—Psalm 63:1

So we stuff ourselves till we're full and we're filled, but we're still not fulfilled. When Gulliver describes the habits of humans to a race of eminently sensible aliens, they are amazed to learn "that we ate when we were not hungry, and drank without the provocation of thirst." And in affluent societies we have the resources to push the experiment to the limit, gorging ourselves not only on food, but on clothes, cars, and toys of all kinds.

Thus "(I Can't Get No) Satisfaction" is the anthem not only of a great rock 'n' roll band, and not only of the restless '60s generation, but of the human condition itself.

As children we press our noses up against the toy store window, peering at our object of desire—the Flexible Flyer sled, the Barbie doll—and imagine that if only we could have that one toy, that would be . . . *It!* Significantly, we never define *It. It* is, in fact, the undefinable satisfaction that we sense must be available somewhere, somehow. (Perhaps we vaguely picture ourselves sledding through the climactic moments of some epic movie, Flexibly Flying over the horizon, silhouetted against a brilliant sunset, as violins swell in orgasmic crescendo.) Children who never get the shiny toy may grow up to butt their heads perpetually against that frustration. But in America, most of us get what we want. Then what?

The thrill is gone.
—B. B. KING

For a few weeks or months, Barbie really does seem to be *It.* But then we get itchy again. If only I could get *Malibu* Barbie . . . If only I could get Ken and Skipper and Miko . . . If only I could get the Barbie Convertible . . . If only I could get the Barbie

Dream House . . . The toys get bigger and more expensive as **I try and I try and I try and I try**, and they're all great as far as they go, but none of them goes all the way. If only I could get into Princeton . . . If only I could get into the corner office . . . If only I could get into bed with that warm, life-size Barbie (or Ken). That would be *It!* Commercial culture has always worked by exploiting this hunger, from Dinah Shore's mid-1950s jingle, "Life is sweeter, it's completer, in a Chevy," to this week's mail-order catalog, each page offering the ultimate gadget, the one so impossibly neato-keen that it will make my head explode. Whoever dies with the most toys wins. But wins what?

Our pleasures and possessions are like ice cream cones: brightly colored, seductively sweet, and, from the first moment, already melting. They're like gaily wrapped Christmas presents, but we've been through enough Christmas mornings to know the sweet anticipation (as long as they're still wrapped, they could still be *It*) and the secret, bitter aftertaste (no matter how good the stuff is, it's after all just stuff). We live in a world of objects and events, goods and services; but somehow no goods deliver The Goods, no services render The Service we want rendered. What's left but to try more positions?

It's this failure to deliver satisfaction that has led some spiritual traditions to condemn worldly pleasures. But there's nothing actually "bad" or sinful about them—they just don't work. As we've seen, *amartia,* sin, merely means "off the mark." What's "sinful" about worldly pleasure is simply that it doesn't hit the spot, and it can distract us from the spot if we fixate on it. Wealth is wonderful. It can buy comfort; it can buy delight; but it can't buy de light. Beyond a certain point, those worldly pleasures just don't get us off. As in the old reefer-madness movies, we find ourselves back at the school yard, pleading with the neighborhood pusher: "Joe, Joe, I need something stronger—Flexible Flyers don't do it for me anymore!"

Hence the quiet, slow-motion panic in the eyes of certain leisured ladies who spend their days in the department store, shopping for satisfaction, never quite finding which department it's in. Or in the eyes of certain outwardly successful gentlemen: *I did everything and got everything they said would make me happy. Now what? Maybe if I trade in all my rusty old toys for some shiny new ones . . . Maybe if I trade in my rusty old bedmate for a shiny new one . . .*

Which brings us to a central theme of the Stones song: sex as a proposed solution to dissatisfaction. That we procreate by entering an ecstatic state is certainly one of the more astonishing bonuses of human life, apparently unique in the animal kingdom. But sexual ecstasy is oversold and overburdened; we see it as our one shot at bliss. In that one fragile basket we place all our eggs (or sperms, as the case may be), putting impossible pressure on our partner *(It must be her fault I'm not happy!)* and on ourself *(Was I good?).* It don't take no Dr. Ruth to tell us that such pressure precludes the relaxed, loving playfulness that makes even sexual happiness possible. Thus the proliferation of books and videos promising fulfillment through Olympic-class erotic technique. (Try more positions indeed.) But if sex is our ultimate happiness, when beauty and potency fade it must leave us in despair. And even in the bloom of sexual vigor, even at the moment of orgasm, a still small voice may whisper, "This is very fine, but it isn't It."

The quest for fulfillment, which sex impersonates (sometimes very convincingly), is the elemental, driving force of all life, expressed so powerfully in the insistent, erotic rhythm of this song's chorus. The near-incomprehensible lyrics of the verses work by transcending specificity; what filters through Jagger's frantic jabber is a portrait of the hot and bothered organism seeking here, there, everywhere, through the entire world of goods and services, bodies and positions, for the orgasmic *Ahhh!* that will make everything all right forever. But because every*where* means every location in the time-space universe of bounded objects and events, and because our hunger for fulfillment is boundless, any such search must fail. And it's not just material possessions and sexual positions that are unsatisfying either. It's also the more sophisticated seductions of political positions, philosophical positions, positions of power, even "spiritual" positions.

But within the structure of that problem is a hint at its solution. The very fact that we have a notion of satisfaction, and feel that there's something wrong with not getting it, means we intuitively know satisfaction, and know it is our birthright—perhaps even our nature.

> *What is the ground of this uneasiness of ours; of this old discontent? What is the universal sense of want and ignorance, but the fine innuendo by which the soul makes its enormous claim?*
>
> —EMERSON

Limitless craving implies a limitless craver. If we can just leave off pursuing unsatisfying objects and rest within our own limitlessness, perhaps satisfaction can be found there. By relinquishing all positions and reposing in positionlessness, we find that we can't *get* satisfaction because we *are* satisfaction. We've been going through life substituting values for x in the equation $x = It$, till one day we discover that "Tag, *you're* It." Then *everything* is satisfying, including the doll and the sled, the goods and the services, and the absence thereof. At last we realize the ironic promise of Jagger's double negative: *can't* get *no* satisfaction means we can't *avoid* satisfaction.

If there is an Infinite, by definition there can't be anyplace where it is not. (If it were everywhere in the universe except the dot over this *i,* it wouldn't be infinite.) So every ounce of the unfulfilling finite must somehow be infinite fulfillingness in drag. We just have to get it out of that odd costume, surprise it in the raw. But whatever skillful means we use to do that, they've got to be *real.* Let's not settle for being Three-Inch Mystics, whose spirituality travels only the distance from their eyes (which read the books) to their mouths (which talk the talk). Like aroused lovers, we've got to dedicate ourselves to entering and being entered by the One, just as determinedly as we tried and we tried and we tried and we tried to get it on with the many. To give satisfaction, the experience of the Infinite has to pierce through our skin and surge through our blood more powerfully than nicotine or heroin, money or sex.

25. Love and marriage

Love and marriage, love and marriage,
Go together like a horse and carriage.
This I tell ya, brother,
Ya can't have one without the other.

Love and marriage, love and marriage,
It's an institute you can't disparage.
Ask the local gentry
And they will say it's elementary.

Try, try, try to separate them,
It's an illusion;
Try, try, try and you will only come
To this conclusion.

Love and marriage, love and marriage,
Go together like a horse and carriage.
Dad was told by mother
You can't have one,
You can't have none,
You can't have one without the other.
—Lyrics by Sammy Cahn,
music by James Van Heusen

*T*ODAY, MANY YOUNG people know this song only as the ironic theme for "Married, With Children," the mutant grandchild of "Father Knows Best" and "Leave It to Beaver," with its aggressively dysfunctional American family. But even in this age of postmodern cynicism, **Love and marriage** still **Go together like a horse and carriage.** Separately, the structurelessness of love is wild, omnidirectional horsepower; the structure of marriage is a stalled carriage that merely provides some cramped, static shelter. Together, they trot down the road of spiritual growth like energy and matter, verb and noun, emptiness and form. **Ya can't have one without the other.**

Love, we're told, will conquer all, resolving all the obstacles to successful marriage. There's great confusion, however, about what love is, how it feels. Our notions of romantic love, derived mainly from movies, pop songs, and advertising, are misleading: we expect a perpetual state of thunderbolt passion, backed up by a guarantee of consumer satisfaction in which our mate fulfills all the categories on our checklist. (Dennis Rodman bod—check! James Dean cool—check! Mister Rogers heart—check!) But beyond any such expectations is a quiet sense that somehow we two belong together; perhaps even that this is a person to whom I can bind myself in my growth toward boundlessness. As in meditation, the kingdom of heaven is not realized through specific flashy experiences: it's not about the epically mind-blowing night of hot sex or even the lyrically heart-melting day of gazing into each other's eyes, although it certainly may include both. As in meditation, it's about hanging out in the simplicity of Being—but together.

Approached in this way, marriage is a most efficacious path of spiritual development, a socially sanctioned opportunity to explore the possibility of loving without limit, which is synonymous with gaining enlightenment, with knowing God. Thus, after saying that loving God with all our heart, soul, and mind is the most important commandment, Jesus adds, "And the second is like unto it, Thou shalt love thy neighbor as thyself." In other words, Instruction #1 is to open to infinite Beingness with every component of my personality, and Instruction #2, *which is equivalent to #1* ("like unto it"), is to open in the same way to the person standing beside me. "Love thy neighbor as thyself" is usually construed to mean loving him *as much as* myself. But "as yourself" can mean something even more challenging—recognizing that he *is* myself, which is true only in that we're both godhead, buddha-nature, Brahman. Marriage gives me a permanent "neighbor," someone who's always close by so that I can keep opening more and more deeply to her on the level where she and I and the Infinite are one.

This is why we speak of *falling in love*. To *fall* is to trip, to sink, to lose our footing as separate selves. (One of the best things about practicing a martial art like Aikido is that you lose your fear of falling; you find out that it's not only okay, it's positively liberating to let go of verticality and get knocked on your ass.) *In* implies that love is somewhere "in here," in the kingdom of heaven within, not "out there" in a landscape of objects and people seen as separate from us. Our lover is someone outside who puts us in touch with what we already are inside. And the *love* into which we fall is unconditional openness. When we say we love someone or something (my wife, my teacher, chocolate mousse cake, Monet's haystacks), we are describing something external that makes us feel serene enough to leave off external striving, to relax into the natural luminosity of our own Being. Unconditional openness is both the method and the result.

There is also a time dynamic to this process. In the early, Romeo-and-Juliet phase, the emphasis is on the dramatic *falling*. Later the emphasis is on *in*: having fallen, we're now in this nice warm cozy place, where no such dramatic motion is required. Later still, it's just *love*—everywhere, undifferentiated, no question of inside or outside.

Never mind that most couples don't fully exploit these cosmic possibilities. The very structure of marriage is such that they'll realize the structureless infinitude of love to whatever degree they're capable in a given moment or lifetime. That's why **It's an institute you can't disparage.** Even the most limited available talent, the yokels of **the local gentry**, can spy the transcendent mystery of love through the magnifying glass of marriage and, like that most sophisticated of detectives, pronounce it **elementary**, Watson. (The growing interest in the institution on the part of gay couples is testimony to its great power. Straight couples might wisely feel that every vote for marriage strengthens their own.)

Try, try, try to separate them. Well, we certainly do. Some people claim that living together is the same thing, that marriage is "just a piece of paper." But in most cases, unless there's commitment there's a holding back; when the escape hatch is open we can't love freely, knowing that the more we give of ourselves the more we'll get hurt if we split.

Love binds to liberate.
—MAHARISHI MAHESH YOGI

Something happens when we take that leap into eternity together. Eternity doesn't merely mean loving for an inconceivably long stretch of time. Love *is* eternity, and eternity is now. By leaping hand-in-hand into the moment (wholeheartedly, without reservations about the past or escape clauses for the future), by taking that Lovers' Leap (suicidal to the bounded self), we can experience the quality of the eternal present which is the essence of enlightenment. That's what the violins and sunsets in movie love scenes hint at.

But violins and sunsets can be misleading if we take them too literally. To expect an unvarying *fortissimo* of romantic passion is to invite big trouble. In real-life, noncinematic marriage, sometimes things are passionate, sometimes they're cosmic, sometimes they're comic, sometimes they're grim. Moods may change along with the sunspot cycle, the menstrual cycle, the business cycle. For days our spouse is like part of the furniture—we barely see her at all—and suddenly we're stammering in disbelief: Has this goddess whom I love so wildly been right here all along?

There's a lesson here about our perception of *everything*. Because marriage is a model of the universe, it's a chance to cultivate the perception of the "one taste" in all the diversity of experience. There's a streak of something subtle, stable, and silent running through all the changes of marriage; it resembles the something subtle, stable, and silent running through all the changes of existence. Marriage attunes us to the changeless by putting us through changes; it attunes us to the deep perfection of all things by exposing us to the surface imperfections of our partner and making it too inconvenient to look for surface perfection elsewhere.

As we gradually let go of all the people we thought our partner was (which were just our concepts) and all the people we wanted her to be (which were just our desires), we start to see who she *is,* which is far more interesting than our desires or concepts. Eventually we give up wondering whether to throw her back: for better or for worse, she's a keeper. The marriage vow, by settling this issue once and for all, settles the mind, making marriage a form of meditation. If we let it, it trains us to stop wondering whether to throw *life* back—it trains us to find the perfection of life as is.

Suggestions for further practice:

- Meditate (in whatever way works for you—silent sitting, devotional singing, etc.). How anyone stays married without spiritual practice is a mystery to me. Living together in the same space without making each other nuts can be difficult; our boundaries inevitably rub against each other, and if all we have is boundaries the rubbing can be intolerable. The cure is to open to boundlessness regularly.

• Take a walk together every day. (In our neighborhood, my wife and I are known as the crazy couple who walk in driving blizzards, pouring rain, parching heat . . .) Aside from promoting the flow of mood-enhancing endorphins, walking ensures that you get time to hash things out. It's different sitting in a room—tensions ricochet off walls and intensify instead of dissipating into the atmosphere. Also, because the right hand naturally swings forward with the left foot and vice versa, walking harmonizes the functioning of the two cerebral hemispheres, producing a clear, tranquil frame of mind: problems seem less overwhelming and solutions present themselves more readily.

• Henry Kissinger once explained the secret of his diplomatic success: always leave the other party room to compromise without losing face. If your position is "No, you're wrong, stupid," then your partner can't budge without admitting stupidity. Also, much needless confrontation can be avoided by using the passive voice, as in "The blanket got pulled over to your side of the bed." Avoid accusations, especially those beginning with the phrase "You always . . ." Find ways to let your partner be right.

• Some understanding of the basic constitutional types outlined by Ayurveda (India's ancient holistic health science) can be extremely helpful. If you know your wife is a *pitta,* or fire type, and she's been doing heavy yard work on a hot July day, you won't take it personally if she flares out at you—it's her inflamed *pitta* talking. Postpone all substantive conversation till she has chilled (literally) with a cold shower and beverage. If your husband is a skinny, airy *vata* type, when he starts feeling nervous and insecure ground him with some warm, rich comfort food.

• Take advantage of the Instant Karma Feedback System built into marriage, which constantly shows us which of our words and deeds are sane and constructive, which are not. (It is the lack of such a system that can make longtime singles so screwy.) The law of karma means there's no free lunch; all our actions have consequences. Anytime we think we can get away, just this once, with being cruel or indifferent or a wisenheimer, it comes back to us one way or another, just because we have to live in the same universe that we're polluting. With a spouse in the loop, it comes back to us quicker. Good karma flows back to us as well—every ounce of kindness we pour upon our partner flows back as nectar upon our own heads.

• **Dad was told by Mother**. Attention, gentlemen: most women intuitively understand all these matters better than you do. Your best bet is to submit quietly to their superior wisdom and not make them get tough with you.

26. (How much is that)
Doggie in the window

How much is that doggie in the window,
The one with the waggly tail?
How much is that doggie in the window?
I do hope that doggie's for sale.

I must take a trip to California
And leave my poor sweetheart alone.
If he has a dog he won't be lonesome,
And the doggie will have a good home.
       —BOB MERRILL

✳

*D*OES A DOG have buddha-nature? The mind-blowing fundamental tenet of Zen is that *everything* has buddha-nature—that "not just illumined sages but all structures of relativity are dwellers in boundlessness" (Prajñaparamita Sutra). As soon as we accept that radical idea, however, we domesticate it—it becomes just another idea, another way to nod our heads sagely and resist having our minds blown. So when a student once asked if a dog has buddha-nature, the wily Zen master Joshu answered *"Mu!* Not!"

Is **that doggie in the window** man's best friend, or a sleeping dog that we'd best let lie? Perhaps, like Joshu's dog, it's an object of contemplation, a springboard for the dive into satori. It begins as a commodity on display, one more alluring consumer good enticing us to press our noses against the glass in the escalating cycle of desire-satiety-disappointment-desire. All those products are so seductive—they sure *look* like man's best friend. The window is awareness, through which we assume we look "out" (from "in" where?) upon the world. But as we've seen, awareness is like a mirror, which reflects all the forms placed before it yet never assumes any of those forms; it never loses its unconditioned purity, even as it reflects a universe of changing conditions. The doggie in the window is a doggie in a mirror.

How much, then, becomes a crucial question, one that the lyric leaves tantalizingly unanswered. The price we pay for the doggie is the price the mirror pays when it decides it's hungry and tries, impossibly, to snatch at the objects paraded before it. Then we're like a dog ourselves, the one in Aesop's fable, which starts across a bridge gripping a juicy bone in its jaws but loses it by snapping at the illusory, insubstantial bone it sees reflected in the stream. The illusion is that there are solid, satisfying "objects" on the other side of the window that can somehow be "had"—and that there's anyone at home on this side of the window to have and be satisfied by them.

Constantly reinforcing that illusion is a commercial economy devoted to keeping us attached and addicted. The doggie we're inquiring about is **The one with the waggly tail**, the seductive, hypnotic waggle exploited by all the home shopping channels as they steadily undulate that cubic zirconia: *You are growing sleepy . . . You are coming under my power . . .* Shake yo' money maker, little doggie! An aspiring rock singer recently told a reporter about his search for just the right distinctive swish of the hand that would seduce the audience's imagination and make him a star. We have products and stars whose success is based on little more. Our supposedly materialistic culture is built not on material at all but on a complex net of such waggles and swishes, artfully designed to snare our attention and our longing. Our children learn early that a burger is not a burger but is the aura and myth of the action hero whose action figure comes in the box with the burger. Our sneakers are not sneakers but are the endorsing athlete's sly smile and graceful slo-mo flight toward the basket. Oh, God, how I want the youth, the power, the self-confidence that Michael's sneakers promise! How I want the bikini paradise of perfect breasts and bottoms that your beer promises! **I do hope that doggie's for sale!**

But suddenly our trance is broken as we remember that we are on a mission, a journey. **I must take a trip to California.** In 1953, when I was a four-year-old in a Levitt tract house on Long Island, Patti Page's recording of "Doggie in the Window" was the first radio song whose lyrics I worked to understand. The most mysterious word was "California." I had no idea what or where California was, but the name evoked a mythic land, a shimmering, transcendent Shangri-La of the imagination. Fourteen years later, in the Summer of Love, thousands of young seekers my age swept into California, where they took a trip indeed. Was the national psyche programming itself in '53, setting a crucial cultural alarm to ring in '67, when it would be time to shake off Eisenhower/tranquilizer slumbers with the crash and flash of Hendrix/acid awakenings? Was this seemingly saccharine-square bit of doggie doggerel really the early-morning muezzin's cry, summoning the most adventurous members of a generation on a pilgrimage to psychedelic Mecca? The journey changed us deeply. Even if it has taken a few decades, we have come to understand that the promise of cosmic Peace and Love which seemed at the time to be encapsulated in a place called California (and encapsulated in pharmaceutical capsules) is actually available everywhere, always. Our only mistake was to think it was as simple as taking a pill; actually it's much simpler.

Hence in this second stanza the narrator (let's call her Patti) makes an abrupt shift. In a moment of clarity she suddenly realizes: I can't keep hanging around here being hypnotized by waggling consumer goods. I must fulfill my cosmic destiny; I must transcend; I must take a trip to California. But then I'll have to **leave my poor sweetheart alone.** If I just disappear in a poof of rainbow light, if I awake into effulgent emptiness, who will take my place in this dream of forms? Who will assume my little piece of the Gross National Product, do my bit to keep the wheels of production and consumption churning? And who will keep my poor sweetheart company? This is an especially poignant question for spiritually aspiring women. Unless they are strongly determined, the resistance of skeptical husbands or boyfriends can be a major stumbling block. Even cultures that venerate crazy wisdom masters may ostracize crazy wisdom mistresses. Men can get nervous about being married to holy women; if our wives become realized sages, will they still cook for us, sleep with us, listen patiently to our grumbling and prattling?

At last the song's real problem has been stated, and in the next moment comes the dazzlingly brilliant solution: **If he has a dog he won't be lonesome.** Patti, it turns out, is not the one being seduced by the doggie. She's going to use it to seduce her mate. First she's going to buy a few of those shiny products in the window (a dishwasher, a television); they will to a certain extent take her place, buying her some time off from the age-old woman's work (cleaning, entertaining) that is never done, time off to become a person, perhaps an enlightened one. If we navigate skillfully enough through the world of forms—if we use them rather than being used and hypnotized by them—they can be our means of liberation.

Second, as Patti gains enough freedom from physical drudgery to explore the mind's pure, mirrorlike nature, she gains a new view of the physical body that drudges—she realizes that she is not it. She sees that what we call our body is merely part of the heap of impressions reflected in the mirror, not the mirror itself; it is part of what's seen through the window, not the seer. Our body, in short, is the dog. *We* are buddha-nature. The dog does not *have* (own, control, master) buddha-nature. Buddha-nature *is,* spontaneous and unborn, perpetually free no matter what the dog does. The awakening of awareness to its own inherent freedom does not conflict with the body's mundane responsibilities.

So, decides our heroine, when I journey to California, to my Shangri-La of transcendence (which is not some far-out, far-western state but a far-in mental state), in my place I will leave one seductive object from the seductive object-world: my body. The dilemma is resolved. My liberated goddess-mind dances in the California sunshine, while my dog-body stays right here with my sweetheart, slogging through the snows of Long Island. Jesus, when asked whether paying taxes to Caesar's Rome conflicts with spiritual freedom, points to Caesar's face on a coin:

> *Render therefore unto Caesar the things which are Caesar's, and render unto God the things that are God's.*
>
> —MATTHEW 22:21

We can satisfy everyone—boss, taxman, sweetheart—by rendering unto them on their own level, while remaining free on *our* level, the God level, buddha-nature level. Thus *moksha* ("liberation") is one of the most potent names for enlightenment. Because form is emptiness, the world of responsibilities cannot weigh us down; its weight is weightless. Because emptiness is form, our open-ended, openhearted, liberated buddha-nature continually generates creative, compassionate ways to fulfill those responsibilities. Be cosmically, act locally.

The doggie will have a good home. So the song has a happy ending. God's in his heaven (the kingdom within), doggie's in the house, all's right with the world. We have co-opted the doggie, converted it from tail-waggling subverter of enlightenment to obedient supporter of enlightenment, just as Padmasambhava converted the hostile demons to guardians of the Dharma-teachings. A second, less well-known translation of Joshu's "Mu!" is "Woof!" Perhaps Joshu is showing the student that everyone, including Zen masters, must interact through the dog-body . . . and that that's fine. Mu—we're dog-gone!

27. *The worms crawl in*

Never laugh when the hearse goes by,
For you may be the next to die.
They wrap you up in a big white sheet
And bury you down about six feet deep.

You're A-OK for about a week,
But then your coffin begins to leak.
The worms crawl in, the worms crawl out,
The worms play pinochle on your snout.

Then a big black bug with beady eyes
Crawls in your liver and out your eyes.
And then you turn a luscious green,
And pus comes out of your ears like cream.

So never laugh when the hearse goes by,
For you may be the next to die!

✳

*J*WAS SEVEN when I realized I was going to die. I
had had no spiritual training; my parents, who were
vaguely atheists, could offer no reassuring words, no comforting
visions of afterlife. I would lie awake nights in a state of terror,
picturing myself planted under the ground with everyone else
walking around over my head. The phrase "And the world will
go on without me" would resonate ominously in my mind.
Finally I would fall asleep out of sheer exhaustion. Once,

when my parents were out, I ran, panicked, down the street in my pajamas to take refuge at the home of some puzzled neighbors.

Meanwhile in Tibet, boys my age, monks in training, were building their own coffins and sleeping in them every night.

Never laugh when the hearse goes by, says this classic of childhood lore, **For you may be the next to die.** For us to keep living, millions of biological processes and environmental conditions have to keep going right, moment after moment. We are perpetually perched on the edge of any one of their going wrong. So never laugh away the imminence of death—it's never more than one heartbeat away, one doze behind the wheel away, one breath away. Significantly, the word *expire* means both to breathe out and to die. Every outbreath is a preview of coming destructions, a tentative death till we breathe in again, and one time we won't.

But usually we're busy denying death. We have some wonderfully evasive expressions for this purpose, like "If something happens to me . . ." It ain't *if,* it's *when,* and it ain't *something,* it's *curtains.* But as we get older and lose more of our friends, denial gets harder. Our denial strategy, like the coffin in the song, **begins to leak.** Walking down a city sidewalk, we may reflect that a hundred years from now, when this shift has retired, the sidewalk will be crowded with new guys, bustling about as if *they're* going to live forever, as indifferent to our former glory as those worms that **play pinochle on your snout.**

My! People come and go so quickly here!
—DOROTHY, IN *The Wizard of Oz*

So perhaps we start looking at death a little more full-on, to see what we can learn from it. (When the Buddha is asked what mentor has given him his great wisdom, he replies, "Death is my guru.")

Until we accept death, we can't fully live life. This is not a poetic sentiment but a precise description of some fundamental mechanics of consciousness. Living life fully (that is, in enlightenment) requires letting go fully. We can't do that as long as there's even a small corner of our awareness where we're trying to hold together the impermanent body-mind structure in an illusion of permanence. At every moment we strive (even unconsciously) to fend off death, to keep from flying apart into a chaos of nonexistence—ultimately a doomed project, of course. As if haunted by our lack of a solid, permanent self, we struggle for self-preservation through a variety of neurotic habits: defending our opinions as if our lives depended on it, feeling threatened by people who look different from us, stubbornly resisting sensible change, demanding a constant flow of stimulation to prove to ourselves that we're still here. (Keep that TV playing day *and* night!)

The solution, demonstrated so brilliantly in this song, is to take a two-pronged approach: first, to visualize clearly and unflinchingly the most grisly details of our physical destruction—**And then you turn a luscious green,** etc.—and, second, to transcend to a larger perspective, from which our destruction doesn't matter. The irony of the admonition to **Never laugh when the hearse goes by** is that when we hear this song we *do* laugh; it's as funny as it is gruesome. By making us laugh at death, it relaxes us enough to take death seriously—to not laugh it off.

In this way the song parallels the Vajrayana Buddhist practice known as *chö* (literally, "cutting"). Tibetans traditionally practiced this form of meditation in the most frightening settings available, preferably the charnel grounds, amid the sights and smells of decomposing corpses in various stages of being broken apart or burned. The chö practitioner invites the demons of the charnel ground to feast on his flesh and blood, which have been transformed into divine nectar. In his imagination he assists with stripping the meat from his own bones, cooking it up in a skull-cauldron the size of the universe, and dishing out portions to the guests. He can also summon up all the most horrible acts of violence that could ever happen to him, visualizing each one as realistically as possible. (In modern practice, we might confront our modern fears by having subway trains run over us, sadistic muggers torture us, tractor-trailers splinter our spines, our limbs lopped off by chainsaws, our heads caught in heavy machinery, battery acid poured down our throats, etc.) The key is to regard all the visions as absolutely real, as actually happening right now.

Chö practice also includes inviting everyone to whom we owe karmic debts—former spouses, business partners, enemies, relatives, anyone we've ever injured in past or present lives—to come and collect. So, still regarding the experience as 100-percent real, we serve up cash, real estate, whatever our creditors might demand as they feast on our flesh. Then, in the final (and crucial) phase of chö, the practitioner remembers that all these horrors have been only a mental creation, taking place within awareness. Whew!

The great power of chö is directly proportional to the great urgency with which we usually fear and deny death. To accept and even to rejoice in one's own destruction (to cry out to the demons, "Okay—gimme your best shot!") is so profoundly liberating that at one point in Tibetan history, it is said, the monasteries were virtually cleared out as monks and nuns abandoned conventional training to seek out chö masters. Nowadays we may be seeking a similar exorcism through horror films. Sitting before the big screen in the darkened theater, we become completely lost in the maimings and killings—as if they're really happening, and happening to us. Then we walk out to the street and again remember it was only a movie, taking place within awareness. Whew!

But, powerful though it is, chö is still an ancillary technique to support simple meditation, the fundamental practice of relaxing into our true nature. Meditation and dying are intimately connected. The Tibetan Book of the Dead and analogous teachings from other cultures give highly detailed guidance for handling the dying process in a way that is most expansive and liberative: they are required reading. But since we **may be the next to die** (perhaps before we get to the bookstore), here's the short version:

Let go, and remain aware.

This may well sound difficult. When we've completely identified with our bodies and personalities, to let go, to let them slip away, sounds like succumbing to a terrifying annihilation. But if we've been meditating regularly, then alert letting go is second nature. We have experienced again and again that when we let go of all the impressions of the mind and senses, including this constellation of impressions we call the body, we come to rest in our own natural boundlessness, the Awareness-Space within which impressions appear and vanish. Through self-inquiry we have looked for the "owner" of that skylike Vastness and found that there is none. By playing "Knock-Knock," we've discovered who's there—nobody. When nobody's there, who's there to die?

> *It's not that I'm afraid to die, I just don't want to be there when it happens.*
>
> —WOODY ALLEN

As it turns out, Woody gets his wish.

So all our meditative practices are also practice for dying. When the death drama starts to unfold, when we get our cue and it's time to say, "Th-th-th-th-th-th-th-that's all folks!" we don't want to find ourselves suddenly thrust onstage without benefit of rehearsal. Conversely, we can use death to support our meditation practice, as an aid to letting go completely. Each time we sit, we can cheerfully assume that we'll die right there on the cushion, so we don't have to bother rehashing the argument we had today or worrying about what to cook for supper tonight.

Of course, once we've realized enlightenment we don't have to bother much about either meditating *or* dying. Then we unshakably know ourselves as the selfless No-thing, the eternal Dreamer within which dreams of selves and things appear and dissolve; as the empty screen upon which it's *all* only a movie. (Whew!) This leaf falls to the ground, this candle sputters out, this body stops breathing—but what does any of that have to do with us? When death comes to the masters, they greet it warmly, as an old friend—one that comes to deepen and widen the master's liberation.

> *Four and fifty years*
> *I've hung the sky with stars.*
> *Now I leap through—*
> *What shattering!*
> —DEATH POEM OF ZEN MASTER DOGEN

The real victory is this joyous shattering, not some cryonic preservation or miraculous resurrection. The real miracle is to know that it's fine *not* to be resurrected, and to dance through every moment with life on one arm and death on the other, finding them both graceful, gracious partners.

SUGGESTIONS FOR FURTHER PRACTICE:

• As described above, meditate like you're dying. Also live like you're dying. (You are.)

• Use the universality of mortality to clarify and simplify your ethics. Just treat everyone like they're dying. (They are.)

• Be with dying people (or rather, since we're all dying, with people who are in the acute stages). Your easy, natural attitude can be a tremendous comfort; you may be the only one among the friends and family not perpetuating denial, willing to talk and listen compassionately but matter-of-factly, and thus help them sort out their feelings. But most important is your ability to just be—to share your own awareness as the open, luminous field within which dying, like everything else, simply happens.

When my mother was dying, I flew to California to be with her, clutching a satchelful of books and tapes on conscious dying. They did prove useful in sparking some moments of insight, but mostly I wound up learning from my mother, from her courage and her humor. (When I played her a tape in which Ram Dass quotes Emmanuel—"Death is like taking off a tight shoe"—her eyes lit up and she exclaimed, "Or a *girdle!*") One afternoon she suddenly felt that she was slipping away: "I think this is it." She had me phone my siblings, who jumped into their cars and raced across town. By the time they got to the house, though, she was feeling better, if somewhat sheepish at having raised such a fuss. What to do now? Well, we decided, everybody's here—let's get some beer and pizza and have a party. The theme: "Excuse me for living!"

When someone close to us dies, it's healthy and necessary to grieve, but somewhere beyond or beneath the grief something remarkable happens if we let it. The dead person's absence, the hole she leaves in the physical world, is an opening into the transcendent, and we can peek into that opening. In the subtlety of our attention we can follow her into the Vastness, as we follow the sound of a bell fading into silence or a flock of birds vanishing into the sky. As my mother was dying, I was naturally focused on this localized being we called Amelia. Then suddenly she was gone—delocalized. In that moment, I somehow saw that she had never really been localized. The appearance of her localization (and mine) had simply given us a way to interact for some years. Now her bursting out of the strictures of that appearance, like taking off a tight shoe (or a girdle), helped me to see what lay beyond it. This was her parting gift.

28. *Hey, hey we're the Monkees*

Hey, hey we're the Monkees,
People say we monkey around,
But we're too busy singin'
To put anybody down.
　　—TOMMY BOYCE AND BOBBY HART

※

MANY PEOPLE were startled when the Copenhagen Zoo recently added a new exhibit between the baboons and the lemurs: a pair of Homo sapiens. But let's face it—we're all a bunch of monkeys. We're just a few chromosomes away from the chimpanzees, and just a few more from all those gibbons and macaques and gorillas our parents used to take us to see, swinging through their big cages or swarming over Monkey Island—shrieking, screeching, and chasing one another up and down trees. That's you, me, the President, and the Pope. So **Hey, hey**, instead of carrying it like a shameful secret, why not join together and proclaim it? Say it loud, I'm a primate and I'm proud!

Of course, those few little chromosomes make a big difference, make us capable of achieving great things undreamed of by the monkey brain. But as we achieve them, we bring our jungle heritage with us.

An example from the monkey: The higher it climbs, the more you see of its behind.

—ST. BONAVENTURE

So it's not surprising that **People say we monkey around**. What can we expect from those snooty people, those suits-and-haircuts who work so hard denying their animalism? Monkeying around is *good*. There's a natural exuberance to it that's more honest than a bookshelf full of moody novels, more edifying than three centuries of French philosophy, more uplifting than a month of Sunday school, more fun than . . . well, you know. Why are those people hassling us?

Those who deny their own monkeyness betray a horror of the animal world of blood, fur, claws, and semen; they may even demand a separate day of creation so as to be aloof, antiseptic nonanimals made in the image of an aloof, antiseptic Divine. Such dualistic thinking splits existence into sacred vs. nonsacred, man vs. nature. But because we *are* nature, all our attempts to "conquer" nature sooner or later become attacks on ourselves. If we hold that even one plant or animal, that even one particle of the universe is not fully pervaded by the same Infinite that pervades us (that *is* us), we have limited the Limitless and set off on a course of self-destruction. The cure is to regard everything in nature as a member of the family. From the symmetry of a pinecone to the power of a thunderstorm to the tranquillity *and* blood lust of creatures great and small, we can open to each as an aspect of ourselves, and to ourselves as an aspect of each.

In popular culture, anyway, animal exuberance might seem to have won the day. Ever since the cultural revolution of the '60s (of which the mild-mannered Monkees were among the most deceptively innocuous harbingers), the monkey has been out of the bag. Crotch-grabbing and simulated humping are all over the airwaves. But many who watch or even perform these allegedly uninhibited entertainments are still caught in dualism. Because they see their bumping and grinding as dangerously or deliciously "bad," it is perversely emphasized. The pornographer ("Hey, look—this is dirty!") is the flip side of the prude ("Don't look—that's dirty!"). The simple theme of this song—that *nothing's* dirty, that we angelic apes are just fine as is—eludes both. Those who work overtime at lasciviously obsessing with the monkey-body, as much as those who work overtime at repressing it, are stuck working overtime. As we gain liberation, we quit all that work. We relax, be whatever we are, and dance on.

Still, some of the folks who don't understand this simple moment-to-moment happiness, this free-swinging natural looseness, are going to complain. What's a monkey to do?

The wisdom offered here is to be **too busy singin' / To put anybody down.** Monkeys can't normally do that. Singing is an act that's as joyous as swinging from trees, but it elevates us to a supra-monkey level. Perhaps scientists will discover one day that the key mechanism in the evolution of lower primates into humans was their listening to birdsong and trying to mimic it. This would force their brains to develop the areas that comprehend rhythm and melody, and thus mathematical sense and linear-narrative sense. They would also develop a sense of aesthetics. They would compare notes with their comrades, competing (like jazzers today) in improvisational duels, perhaps incorporating them into their courtship rituals, eventually ensuring the survival of the hippest. In short, they would become human.

Since birds are winged messengers from the sky, this gift of music might also have been seen early on as a connection with something "higher." Singing was a way to connect with that blue expansiveness the birds keep flying in and out of. Gazing at them as they gradually vanished from view might even have been the earliest form of meditation. (*Namkhai naljyor,* or sky-gazing yoga, is still an important Dzogchen practice.) If we could sing like birds, maybe we could somehow soar like birds into some fantastic sky realm. That vision probably inspired us to create winged gods, who in turn helped incite our spiritual longing—and whom we courted, as we courted one another, with song.

Some of our modern problems may be exacerbated by letting others do our singing—on the radio, the TV, the ubiquitous Walkman.

In a great civilization, everyone sings.
—PROFESSOR WILDER BENTLEY, SAN FRANCISCO
STATE COLLEGE, 1967

Something happens when we belt out sounds from our own center, something powerfully invigorating, tranquilizing, healing, balancing. Another announcement scientists will probably make (if they haven't already) is that uninhibited singing promotes the release of endorphins, lowers blood lactate levels, and increases T-cell count.

A hundred years ago, most American homes had pianos in

their parlors (for many years pianos outnumbered bathtubs). Families gathered around the piano and sang every night, commingling their energy and releasing interpersonal tensions. Today many people feel self-conscious about singing in groups, unless first loosened by several cold ones. But maybe you can be as loose as you let yourself, even without benefit of brew.

And maybe you can do *whatever* makes your *life* sing, whether it's riding your motorcycle, painting with your watercolors, perfecting your slap shot, or hiking the Great Smokeys. Life is too interesting to spend it all watching TV, too short to spend it all working. But work can also make your life sing, if you're engaging in what the Buddha called perfect livelihood, what we might call doing the work that makes your eyes light up.

Sometimes *how* you do it is as important as what you do. Once, years ago, I decided my teaching job had become too stifling. I flew out to California, took several interviews, and was convinced that at least one would develop into an offer. But when I came back to New Jersey to finish out the year, something strange happened. Certain that I was leaving, I felt free to monkey around. I decided to forget about departmental evaluations, about what students might tell their parents, about what administrators might think, and teach the way I *wanted* to teach instead of the way I was s'pozed to teach. I started having fun in the classroom, taught whatever seemed fascinating instead of sensible, challenged and shocked my students at every opportunity. I became thoroughly reckless—and had, by far, my best teaching year ever. I also discovered that my feelings of being stifled had been self-imposed. My bosses saw that my new style worked, and they left me alone. I wound up staying where I was.

Behold, I make all things new.
—REVELATION 21:5

If you ever stop playing, you start dying.
—NGAK'CHANG RINPOCHE

If you do everything like there's no tomorrow (which is, in fact, the case), today becomes an exhilarating adventure. People who haven't missed their own adventure rarely feel compelled **To put anybody down** for pursuing theirs. And putting people down always costs—we never get away with it. Lifting people up is always free. Whether the people we're dissing even hear it or not, put-downs poison the atmosphere in which *we* must live; praise and appreciation fill it with light.

SUGGESTIONS FOR FURTHER PRACTICE:

• Sing in the shower every morning—no matter how crummy you feel. In fact, it's when you feel especially crummy that it's most important. Blues, show tunes, Sousa marches—whatever gets your motor running. If you're so moved, sing your favorite mantras or hymns. Try to include high notes and low notes and a full spectrum of vowel sounds ("Oh, say can you see . . ."): each has different vibrational qualities that awaken different aspects of our energy.

Here you're solidly in the tradition of the monks who for thousands of years have done their morning ablutions in the Ganges while singing the praises of the Infinite. There's something especially enlivening about vigorously intoning sounds while immersed in the water element. Do you feel like a fool? Good! Get down and get foolish!

• While you're in the bathroom, you can also loosen up by making faces in the mirror. Monkey faces, monster faces, crazy faces, clown faces, any kind of faces that help keep you from taking yourself too seriously, from getting too stuck in a rigid idea of who you are.

• Always take advantage of group singing situations by singing as loudly and lustily as possible; never worry about singing off-key. Other people *love* it when you sing off-key— it gives *them* permission to relax and cut loose.

• It may take time, but the habit of putting people down can be broken. Even once a day, just as your lips are opening to dish some dirt, instead breathe out and let it go. Meanwhile, keep meditating and keep singing. Monkeying around will save you from becoming an old fart.

• If your spirituality destroys your sense of humor, it's defeating its own purpose. If your regard for holy doctrines or persons make you stiffly pious, something's wrong.

Sacred cows make the tastiest hamburger.
            —ABBIE HOFFMAN

29. Pennies from heaven

Every time it rains, it rains
Pennies from heaven.
Don't you know each cloud contains
Pennies from heaven?

You'll find your fortune falling all over town;
Be sure that your umbrella's upside down.

Trade them for a package of
Sunshine and flowers.
If you want the things you love,
You must have showers.

So when you hear the thunder,
Don't run under a tree,
There'll be pennies from heaven
For you and me.
—JOHN BURKE AND ARTHUR JOHNSTON

✳

J APED TO THE wall over my desk is a cartoon
clipped out of *The New Yorker*. The caption is "Have
a Nice Day!" and the picture shows a yellow Smiley Face . . . in
a guillotine, awaiting decapitation.

Like the Smiley Face and its slogan, this song might seem to
epitomize the most naïve kind of optimism, the dumbest insis-

tence that we live in the best of all possible worlds despite the grimmest evidence to the contrary. But moksha changes everything. Our reaction to that cartoon is a sort of benchmark indicating the distance to liberation. In that state, we defy all the cynics and sophisticates, including ourselves. We *do* have a nice day, even in the guillotine of daily life.

Every time it rains. What is the "it" invoked by such expressions as "It's hot," "It's April," "It figures," "**It rains**"? Interesting grammatical structure, that. Its indeterminacy hints at an unseen, indeterminate Prime Mover behind or within everything that moves. Every drop of rain that rains upon us, every April that Aprils upon us, is a little bundle of the transcendent, the unmanifest Divine precipitating itself into manifestation. **It rains / Pennies from heaven.** Every particle of manifestation—every pebble, cornflake, and galaxy—retains the full glory, the heavenly identity of It, the unmanifest essence (the same It we once hoped Barbie would be—and which in fact she, along with everything else, turns out to be). This is true even of **pennies**—no need to talk of dollars or doubloons. As the penny is the humblest and commonest of coins, even the humblest moments of experience, the commonest objects, embody the Ultimate. (American pennies bear the likeness of Abraham Lincoln, the Great Emancipator, the bringer of moksha-liberation, who insisted that the full dignity of humanity resided even in what was then considered the humblest of races.)

Don't you know . . . ? Can't you see? In the liberated state we're amazed that anyone can fail to notice this most fundamental fact of life, which constantly rains down upon us all. How can anyone remain ignorant even of who they are, sustain the unsustainable feat of binding up boundless Being within the illusory constraints of limitation? To the enlightened, the word "enlightenment" is a joke. There is no special state requiring a special word to denote it. There is only the way things matter-of-factly are: limitlessly, wonderfully okay.

Each cloud contains / Pennies from heaven. Since everything in this world, seen as it is, is nothing but divine glory, that glory must include all that we normally think of as clouds in our sky, as areas of darkness blotting out the light of happiness. Every piece of so-called bad luck, bad karma, bad things happening to good people, is just another drop of Godness falling on our heads. Here enlightenment resolves the Problem of Evil, that dualistic swamp in which so many earnest minds have wallowed and sunk: Why does God allow—or create—suffering? Job, the good man to whom every possible bad thing happens, howls the question at the sky, and from out of the whirlwind (more stormy weather), God answers him with another question: "Where were you when I laid the foundation of the earth?" (This is the Old Testament version of "Show me the face you had before your parents met.") God continues:

> *Where is the way to the dwelling of light? . . .*
> *Have you entered the storehouses of the snow? . . .*
> *Has the rain a father? . . .*
> *Do you give the horse its might? . . .*
> *Is it by your wisdom that the hawk soars? . . .*
> *And can you thunder with a voice like this?*

In all this, God does not answer Job with concepts. Instead, each clause of his elaborate koan (the longest speech in the

Bible) challenges Job to widen his perspective beyond the narrow confines of conceptuality and individuality, to enter into the Vastness that begets earth, light, snow, rain, horse, hawk, Job; to mount into that boundless sky; to see as God sees; to be as God is. From that view, in that state of absolute Reality, there *is* no suffering—there is only openness of Being, flowing frictionlessly within itself. The friction we experience in the toothache and earthquake is the friction of our own resistance to what Is, the resistance that Job finally gives up.

Then he exclaims, "I had heard of you by the hearing of the ear, but now my eye sees you." With the direct vision of satori experience, in the dawning light of gnosis, we find that our darkness has vanished. We are (like Job, whose catastrophes are all reversed at the end of the story) rehabilitated even from the traumas of the past. Mercifully, the experience of the Eternal is retroactive; timelessness heals all wounds.

Amazingly, it's all grace, whether it's peace, war, marriage, divorce, winning the lottery, losing the house, banana split, bed of nails. Of course this proposition defies all logic. Of course on the commonsensible level, as we move through time, we still do everything we can to minimize suffering. But on the uncommon, supersensible level, where we rest outside of time, everything's mellow. On the relative side, we may still complain about our headache and cry at the funeral. But on the absolute side, it's all endlessly fine, including headache and funeral, complaining and crying.

Now I see there is no problem.
—VOICE MAIL FROM A FORMER STUDENT

All this is nothing but That.
—CHANDOGYA UPANISHAD

Here Christianity's central fact and symbol has become its central misunderstanding: Christ's "suffering" on the cross. The confusion is rooted in the word "suffer," which in King James's time meant "to allow" (as in "Suffer the little children to come unto me"). Christ *allowed* the crucifixion; he was taking it as it comes. If he were merely Jesus (a limited personal identity) he would merely experience pain. But he has realized himself as enlightened Christ (the Hindu's effulgent Self, the Buddhist's luminous no-self). To such a realized one, all *this* (hand, nail, nail piercing hand, buzzing fly, sunset, sponge full of vinegar) is nothing but *That* (non-dual Being). It's not a matter of being numb—enlightenment is not some exotic form of novocaine. It's perceiving the waves of pain and the waves of pleasure as waves upon the same ocean of That which both includes and transcends pleasure and pain. Cross, guillotine, root canal . . . we're all having a nice day.

You'll find your fortune falling all over town. Now comes the song's apocalyptic moment. A **town** is a construct, with its matrix of perpendicular streets and avenues, its diversity of buildings, its bustle of people and activities. Here it stands for the matrix of relative life, the web of space and time, cause and effect, history and psychology, all the multiplicity we generate out of essential unity. We call this the world and then lose ourselves in it, seeking our **fortune**. But here comes our *real* fortune (O fortunate us!), our own heavenly nature, in a deluge, **falling** and washing over all the stuff we thought was important and real.

What should we do when this apocalypse comes? Simple: **Be sure that your umbrella's upside down.** The urgency of this one practical step is underlined by the words **Be sure**. An umbrella is normally a shelter from the rain, a little portable roof. It's the turtle shell of selfness, the sense of being a being that is separate from the universe and therefore needs protection from its vicissitudes. Before setting out on the spiritual path, we clung tightly to the self. Once on the path, seeing the need to get all wet in God's deluge, perhaps we thought we needed to destroy the self. But the message here, with enlightenment's advent, is that we don't throw away the umbrella after all. Individuality is not our identity, but it's a necessary part of our equipment; we needn't destroy it just because it's limited, any more than we need to destroy the limited body.

For the liberated, the apparent self is limited but not limiting. It's all how we carry it, and the way to carry it is exactly 180 degrees from how we used to. Just turn it **upside down** (like the Hanged Man of the Tarot deck), so that it's open, receptive. Having accomplished this maneuver, we accept all our circumstances with great good humor, relaxed gratitude, and a personal grace in action that matches the amazing grace that floods upon us from all sides. We become like Sono ("Thank you for everything. I have no complaint whatsoever"), or St. Francis, or Rabbi Carlebach, or Neem Karoli Baba, or the Dalai Lama, of whom we might well say, "*Their* umbrellas are upside down!" Their good humor is further fed by the great joke that people consider them somehow special or unusual. They know they're just living normal life, while others persist in the odd, tragicomic labor of holding their self-umbrellas constantly upright to protect themselves from their own good fortune.

Nor is this enlightenment a state of merely abstract, meta-physical bliss:

Thy kingdom come. Thy will be done on earth as it is in heaven. Give us this day our daily bread.

—MATTHEW 6:10–11

These pennies of heavenly awareness are good bread—practical, durable coin of the earthly realm. We can **Trade them for a package of / Sunshine and flowers,** blessing with our natu-rally sunshiny disposition the lives of those not yet ready for singin' in the rain, and bringing to flower our worldly aspira-tions, which naturally blossom in our fullness of spirit.

Why, then, doesn't everyone invert their umbrellas? What drives people to evade the fullness of their own nature? Noth-ing but fear, the child's fear of the unknown—groundless fear, as it turns out. **So when you hear the thunder, / Don't run under a tree**. Don't look to the ever-branching structures of the material world for the refuge that you couldn't get and didn't need from your so-called self. Don't run from the lightning flash of radically transformative truth. Will it blind you? Sure, but only so that, like St. Paul in the desert, you can truly see. Will it roast you? You bet, but it will roast you to perfection for the Vajra Feast of eternal life. That ominous rumble is just the pre-lude to your own apotheosis. It's God clearing his throat before pronouncing his blessing upon you with the same thunderous voice that Job heard. It's the hot lava of your own subterranean nature, rich with precious ores, getting ready to erupt. And the apotheosis is democratic, universal—these riches belong to every-one: **There'll be pennies from heaven / For you and me.**

30. Let's call the whole thing off

You say eether and I say eyether,
You say neether and I say nyther;
Eether, eyether, neether, nyther,
Let's call the whole thing off!

You like potato and I like potahto,
You like tomato and I like tomahto;
Potato, potahto, tomato, tomahto!
Let's call the whole thing off!

But oh!
If we call the whole thing off, then we must part.
And oh!
If we ever part, then that might break my heart.

So, if you like pajamas and I like pajahmas,
I'll wear pajamas and give up pajahmas.
For we know we need each other,
So we better call the calling off off.
Let's call the whole thing off!

—Words by Ira Gershwin,
music by George Gershwin

W E'RE ALL TALKING about one thing because there's only one thing to talk about. There's just one thing to say about it, and that can't be said.

I gotta use words when I talk to you.
—T. S. ELIOT

The curse of words is that they make the simple seem complicated, like the opaque prose of a software manual that we wade through till we realize, "Ah—just click the mouse *here!*" The blessing of words is that, if used skillfully, they do finally bring us to that simple click. Then it's time to put the manual down.

We stand by the poolside arguing about how to dive. You say half-gainer, I say jackknife, she likes swan dive, he likes cannonball. Whichever way we go, we wind up in the same water. Given the immensity of the Absolute pool and the slipperiness of the relative deck, the miracle is that anyone's still on their feet. If we dance around the edge long enough, eventually we'll fall in. Of course, "eventually" may be thousands of lifetimes, and a perfectly executed jackknife certainly may take us in deeper and faster and less painfully than a belly flop. But we can only do what *we* can do. That cosmic pool itself, speaking in the form of Lord Krishna, says:

As men approach me so do I accept them: men on all sides follow my path.

In other times and places we might be offered only one path of practice and one spiritual vocabulary. The smorgasbord of options spread before literate late-twentieth-century Americans is unprecedentedly lavish. But all systems and doctrines are verbal structures; they are models of the Truth, not the Truth itself. Just as model cars are made of plastic parts, these models of infinite, absolute Reality are made of finite, relative words. All models have limitations and flaws, and words are even less reliable than plastic: their meanings change from culture to culture, person to person, moment to moment. "Heavenly Father" had a different resonance in Jesus' patriarchal society than it does for Americans who see Al Bundy dissed by his wife and kids every week; it has a different resonance for me now than it did when my earthly father was alive.

You say Brahman and I say Allah,
You like ananda and I like heaven,
Moksha, Salvation, Great Spirit, Shunyata,
Let's call the whole thing off!

When, separated by oceans and centuries, Prophet A spoke of God, Prophet B spoke of Vastness, and Prophet C spoke of Voidness, they presumably had no idea that one day a bunch of comparison-shopping Americans would be trying to reconcile their diverse expressions. Coming from different cultural and linguistic backgrounds, A said **potato** and B said **potahto**. Each **liked** (felt comfortable with, and even devoted to) the pronunciation he had inherited or devised. But it's still the same vegetable.

Even pairs of terms that appear diametrically opposed (personal God vs. Impersonal Absolute, fullness of Brahman vs. emptiness of Shunyata) remind us that because the highest Truth is infinite, it's beyond the power of words to define. At the same time, because the highest Truth is infinite, there's plenty of it to go around. So, which description is right? **Eether, eyether, neether, nyther**. No one has the Truth; everyone has the Truth. This can lead to a lot of quibbling:

> *We have just enough religion to make us hate, but not enough to make us love one another.*
>
> —JONATHAN SWIFT

No one's immune. Even in Tibet, rival schools occasionally burned down one another's monasteries; even in merry England, they burned one another at the stake. It's enough to make us give up dialogue entirely. **Let's call the whole thing off!**

But is that really an option now? The world has grown too small for the old luxury of deciding that **we must part**. We can't huddle behind walls of mutual ignorance anymore. **For we know we need each other**—in the new era of interdependent economies and interactional ideologies, we can run but we can't hide. No longer able to pursue a separate peace, we at last have to make peace together.

A useful step might be to acknowledge that all our words are, as they say in Zen, fingers pointing at the moon, and not the moon itself. (Historically, the big problems often start when the pointing fingers become so ornately bejeweled that we fixate on them and forget the moon.) If we could catch It in our verbal net, It would be just another word or concept and so not what we're looking for. The hippest of scriptures acknowledge this: the Tao Te Ching warns in its first sentence that the Tao one can speak of is not the true Tao, and the Prajñaparamita Sutra deconstructs itself on every page.

It's when we *see* that moon—when we're living in the nirvana to which the scriptures refer—that we can say **Let's call the calling off off**: let's resume communication and resolve our doctrinal wrangling. When we're moving our furniture into that kingdom of heaven which we once merely discussed from a distance, we can call off the parlor debates and religious wars. Our descriptions still sound different, but descriptions are no longer all we've got. We can diverge linguistically and converge experientially. We're like people who once fought over whether to call it the Grand Canyon or *el Cañon Grande,* over whose map was better. Maybe mine was prettier; maybe yours got you here faster. (As a word-intoxicated six-year-old, I took a tour with my family through the Grand Canyon and never saw it . . . I was too busy reading the guidebook. Spiritual-book addicts, take heed!) Now, standing at the canyon's rim, peering into it with shared amazement, we know it's *this*—and if I exclaim "Oh, wow!" and you exclaim "*¡Ay, caramba!*" we understand each other well enough. The awesomeness of sacred experience is such that we no longer have the luxury, the available unastonished brain cells, to quibble.

The problem stems largely from setting down in writing the ecstatic proclamations of enlightened holy men and women. These transcriptions usually fall a little flat on paper, like the printed lyrics accompanying rock albums. The spirit, the music that enlivened the words, is missing. But we can re-enliven the songs by singing the lyrics ourselves, and re-enliven the scriptures by experiencing for ourselves the ecstasy from which they proceeded. Then we can gaze at one another in wide-eyed, wordless awe:

> *Why should I flail about with words, when love*
> *has made the space inside me full of light?*
> —KABIR

This doesn't mean we have to abandon our diverse religions and adopt some kind of lukewarm eclectic compromise. Ira Gershwin, who wrote the words to *this* song, was once traveling in England, where he heard a young chorus girl sing it as an audition piece. In her British diction it became, "You like potahto and I like potahto . . ." If it's all potahto, the joke doesn't work. While all teachings are the same on the final level of Absolute attainment, on the provisional level of relative practice they're different, and it's no use trying to cook them into one big mass-consumption potahto soup. *Vive la différence.*

The question is not which teachings are "true," since, as

we've seen, they're all false and all true (and *all* made up). The question is which teachings are useful—for *you*. Which ones talk to you? Which songs and stories inspire you, which explanations make sense to you, which images and traditions take you beyond making sense, which practices will you actually do? Can you practice with no tradition at all? Maybe, just as a great jazz musician—say a Thelonius Monk—may create brilliant music out of pure improvisation. But even a Monk usually needs the structure of a melody or a chord progression, if only as a point of departure toward structurelessness.

So even diverse traditions are really not diverse enough: they merely provide a framework for individual experience. Each seeker's romance with the Infinite is unique. Thus Lord Krishna is said to have manifested 108 bodies, to dance simultaneously with each of the 108 maidens who loved him—each of whom was convinced (correctly) that she was dancing with the *real* Krishna. The 84,000 teachings of the Buddha symbolize the fact that, just as the individual dramas of confusion are innumerable, so are the paths to ultimate clarity. As we say in America, *E pluribus unum*: from a plurality of distinct paths may we reach the Unity beyond distinctions. Then, acknowledging that our intimacy is unavoidable, that we're all in this big bed together, we can put on our **pajamas** (or **pajahmas**) and let the nuptials begin.

When, at last, even our conflicts don't conflict, we can truly call the calling off off. We can agree to disagree, to use different words and concepts to convey our joy at having been ravished by the same word-melting, concept-shattering Divine. Then we can sit together and schmooze like old men in a barbershop debating about beautiful women. You say Greta Garbo and I say

Hedy Lamarr, you like Lana Turner and I like Paulette Goddard. We're delighted to be here, delighted to share our delight in the endlessly diverse forms of the same endless beauty.

SUGGESTIONS FOR FURTHER PRACTICE:

• Whatever the ultimate Reality may be—God, Nothing, Paradox, Paradise, Is-ness, Infinity, Allah, Great Spirit, Love, Light, Question Mark—**OPEN** yourself to it totally.

• **LET GO** of everything, including whatever names or ideas you may have concerning that Reality; including any expectations about what should happen or what you should experience; including how you "do" this opening up. You don't do it—it does you.

• **PERSIST**.

31. *Happy trails*

Happy trails to you
Until we meet again,
Happy trails to you
Keep smiling until then.

Who cares about the clouds when we're together?
Just sing a song and bring the sunny weather.

Happy trails to you
Till we meet again.
—DALE EVANS

✳

*I*SIS AND OSIRIS . . . Shiva and Sati . . . Lord Rama and his paragon of wives, Queen Sita . . . Roy Rogers, King of the Cowboys, and Dale Evans, Queen of the West . . .

Each week, when Roy and Dale crowded their radiant faces together into the TV screen to sing this song at the conclusion of their show, I couldn't imagine a diviner divine couple. Now that it's time to take my leave, I'd like to borrow the words of their cheery benediction and wish **Happy trails to you**.

I hope this book has encouraged you to tread the spiritual trail seriously, but not solemnly. Why get grim about this stuff— why trudge along, investing all our happiness in some hypothetical future, the final square in the Chutes-and-Ladders game, the theoretical Promised Land of enlightenment? The future is always a theory. Reality is always now. Therefore I urge you not to trudge but to dance; it's a happy trail, not just a trail to happiness.

Don't worry that you don't know which way to go:

Whosoever maketh effort for Us, in our ways shall We certainly guide them.

—KORAN

Just start going—maketh effort. The spiritual path is like anything else. If you want, say, to draw, you don't wait till you can see the whole picture. You take pencil in hand, start scribbling or sketching, and the picture eventually emerges from the process. In the same way, you can read books forever and fret about not knowing which advice to follow, or you can do *something,* make some kind of motion. Then you get feedback—you feel either smooth trail or thorny brush beneath your feet, and adjust your direction accordingly.

Stand at the crossroads and look. Ask for the ancient paths and where the best road is. Walk in it, and you will live in peace.

—JEREMIAH 6:16

Until we meet again. One way or another, I'm convinced, we all meet again. Buddhists, who see our lives in the context of innumerable rebirths, say that sooner or later we have every possible relationship to every other being in the universe. From that dizzying array of possibilities, they draw a simple conclusion: Be kind to everyone, because everyone has been your mother. The Dalai Lama says he tries to treat everyone he meets like an old friend. Perhaps everyone we meet actually *is* an old friend.

This business of life, then, this crawling toward some kind of light, is a group endeavor. Jews require a *minyan,* or group of ten, to commune with the Infinite in certain ways, and Native Americans often dedicate their spiritual practice by shouting "*Mitakuye oyasin!* All my relations!"—meaning all beings. We're in this together and must support one another. The stretches of the trail that are dark and fearful, which might overwhelm us individually, grow bright in the light of our mutual lovingkindness: **Who cares about the clouds when we're together? / Just sing a song and bring the sunny weather.**

In fact, there are many who have made this practice of lovingkindness their main activity on the trail. These are the saints and bodhisattvas—the buddhas-in-process who have vowed to liberate all beings, like the heroes who stay in a burning building to help others escape. Compassion for others on the path becomes their path. We can join them anytime.

Although the Bodhisattva Vow looks forward to eventual universal enlightenment, its full force is right now. It changes the way we relate to ourselves, to others, to each moment and what we choose to do in it.

Bodhisattvas never get a vacation.
—H.H. THE FOURTEENTH DALAI LAMA

For starters, it means that the guy who cuts us off on the turnpike, the terrorist who blows up the building, the kids on our nerves, the parents on our case, the fly in our soup: *these* are the beings we have vowed to save with our compassion—liberate them into the loving spaciousness of our awareness. This requires a continual renewal of will and attention. It's far easier to cop out, to veer off the trail of love and go back to the deeply grooved rut of reactivity. If we want to go on hating Hitler, or Mao, or Nixon, or our abusive parent, or our mean English teacher, or the liberals, or the conservatives, that's our privilege. But if we want to be enlightened, at some point we have to learn to love them. If that sounds hard, it is, and it's one of the reasons why most of us are still on the road.

Meanwhile, here are some unwritten traffic rules and motoring tips that may help keep the trail happy for ourselves and others. Like all the advice in this book, it is addressed to myself as much as to anyone else:

• Know in advance that there will always be distractions tempting you to wander off the trail—people and attitudes and ambiences ready to convince you that the pursuit of the Spirit is not important or real.

And be not conformed to this world: but be ye transformed by the renewing of your mind.
—ROMANS 12:2

• Know that proselytizing doesn't work. In our zeal to share the simple truth that will set people free from their complicated suffering, we can wind up turning them off. Like us, they need the space to find it on their own. Besides, the subtlety of real spiritual insight and experience is far too delicate to survive the rude jostling of evangelism. The Tao that can be hawked, hustled, peddled, or coerced is not the true Tao. When we feel the urge to preach, it's good to ask ourselves what need of our own we're addressing. The best preaching is diligence in our practice, to become the best possible example of what this stuff can do. Eventually they'll ask what we've been up to.

For many are called, but few are chosen.
—MATTHEW 22:14

We could even say that all are called but few have chosen *yet.* In time, all will choose the Eternal because there's no other choice, because it's not possible to abide permanently in the impermanent. There are no spiritual or nonspiritual people; everyone is on the trail, some of them consciously.

• Be careful of showing off, of spirituality as a fashion statement. (*Look, everybody! I'm wearing my meditation beads, I'm wearing my meditation shirt, I'm sitting in the lotus pose!*) Jesus knew all about such show-offs: "Verily I say unto you, they have their reward." That is, they get the attention they want instead of the transcendence they need. All the posters and trinkets and other spiritual toys can, however, serve a valid purpose if they're used as a support, rather than a substitute, for genuine spiritual practice—just as playing with a toy doctor's kit might inspire a child to become a real doctor one day.

• Following the famous Middle Way is important, but that doesn't mean being lukewarm or blasé or bland. It means steering clear of both flakiness and self-righteousness by being joyful and conscientious. It means recognizing that the path runs through the middle of every moment, that ultimate Reality is always right here in the middle of everything ("*In mitn derinnen!*" as my father used to shout, with Yiddish exasperation, when the phone rang in the middle of supper). It means recognizing that, because Reality has no beginning or end, we're always in the middle of it—it's not deferred till we get on top of things, or get to the bottom of things. Whatever's swirling around us, we're always at the middle of the mandala, the axle of the action, the hub of the hubbub.

Buddhists signify their entrance onto the path with the Refuge Vow, formally taking spiritual refuge in Buddha (the trailblazer), Dharma (the teachings, the road signs), and Sangha (the fellow wayfarers). Implicit in that vow is the relinquishing of everything else as possible refuges—money, family, friendship, intellect or emotion, optimism or cynicism, sensuality or asceticism. We can't be serious travelers if we're huddled in any of those roadside huts. This doesn't mean abandoning money and friends and the rest; it means abandoning the illusion that they can take us to our goal.

• Remember that it's **Happy trails**, plural. Other people will follow other trails (or other branches of the One Trail). We wish them well and assume that they will have great success. It's good not to be too dogmatic about our views . . . then it's less embarrassing later, when our views change.

All teachings are provisional. Confusion results from trying to make the Bible or the Koran or the Vedas or the Sutras the rock. Even rocks, for that matter, shift and crumble in time;

not even rocks are rocks. If you regard your path as absolute, then—

You will be easily caught by some particular way, and you will say, "This is enlightenment! This is perfect practice. This is our way. The rest of the ways are not perfect. This is the best way." This is a big mistake. There is no particular way in true practice. You should find your own way, and you should know what kind of practice you have right now. Knowing both the advantages and disadvantages of some special practice, you can practice that way without danger. But if you have a one-sided attitude, you will ignore the disadvantage of the practice, emphasizing only its good part. Eventually you will discover the worst side of the practice, and become discouraged when it is too late. This is silly. We should be grateful that the ancient teachers point out this mistake.

—Shunryu Suzuki-roshi

• Nothing that happens to us on the trail is a mistake. Sometimes it's a Yellow Brick Road, sometimes it's a razor's edge. Anything that presents itself as a difficulty is something we need to master on our way to wholeness; otherwise it wouldn't be difficult.

Even moments of delight along the way can be traps if we fixate on them or enshrine them. As children, perhaps we brought home from camp the shiny pebble that we found at the most magical moment of the magical summer. But we're going to move on down the road to moments that are even more magical, which we might miss if we're too busy tending our pebble collection. This brings us back to Blake's challenge:

He who binds to himself a joy
Does the wingéd life destroy.

Now we can understand his solution:

But he who kisses the joy as it flies
Lives in Eternity's sunrise.

• We never know where guidance on this trail is going to come from; sometimes we have to be alert not to overlook it.

Old joke: Two explorers are sitting at a bar in Alaska, disputing whether God exists. The first explorer says, "Well, one time I was trekking alone across the tundra and I lost my compass. I went on for eight days and just got deeper into the frozen wastes. I was out of food and water, and all my toes were frostbitten. Finally I looked up to the sky and said, 'God, if you exist, show me a sign. Do something to get me out of here.'" "Did God answer you?" asks the second explorer. "To tell you the truth, I never found out. Just then some damned Eskimo came along and took me to his village."

• All paths are valid, says Ramana Maharshi, because all paths are illusory. The idea that there are two separate things, ignorance and enlightenment, is absurd (from the point of view of enlightenment!). Equally absurd, therefore, is the idea of a path connecting them. At every step, boundless Reality is beneath our feet. Therefore it makes perfect sense to be happy *on* the trail. It also makes perfect sense to keep walking till we get to the point where we know there was never anywhere to walk. When we realize nothing needs transforming, we're transformed.

For the wise who realize everything as Brahman, what is there to meditate or not to meditate, what to speak or not to speak, what to do or not to do?

—SHANKARA

May we live in Eternity's sunrise. May your heart-mind and my heart-mind remain inseparable. May we all together get to the other side.

Happy trails to you, until we meet again.

Postscript: Love makes the world go round

I SWEAR I'M typing this through my tears.

It's the summer of 1995. I'm on a month-long meditation retreat, high on a hilltop over the Finger Lakes. No TV, no newspapers, almost no conversation. In my absence the American bombers have or have not flown to Bosnia, and the suffering there has lessened or grown. The O.J. jury has fried him or walked him or hanged itself or not. If the *New York Times* falls on my driveway and there's no one there to read it, does it make a sound? CNN beams its signal in vain at my cold TV screen, as blank as the face I had before my parents met. I'm missing from action, a prisoner of peace.

I've just walked back from the meditation hall, where we were chanting *Om mani pédmé hūng,* the Mantra of Great Compassion, pouring out lovingkindness from our hearts to our families, to our enemies, to the world, to all beings throughout the universe. As we chanted, from within vast Awareness-Space made clear and vivid by weeks of intensive meditation, I felt luminous beams of love radiating from my heart center. At the practice leader's suggestion, we directed this force to Bosnia—to Rwanda—to Tibet—to the inner cities of America. Eventually I noticed I was sobbing.

The diplomats and technocrats have had their chance, and we still have war, torture, ecological poisoning. This beautiful planet, on which so much happiness so sporadically blossoms, may be on the brink of becoming uninhabitable. For many people it has already gone over that brink, their fragile niche made a hell realm by others, who, also fearful of suffering and death, exploit a momentary upper hand.

Our sophistication having failed, perhaps it's time (as Buckminster Fuller said) to dare to be naïve—to rely on such inane, starry-eyed wisdom as **Love makes the world go round.** What if that's literally true? What if the joyful clarity we feel in the purest moments of human love is a spark of the blazing Radiance that sets the planets and galaxies spinning like so many brilliant prayer wheels? If love indeed runs the universe, *is* the universe, our failure to love is what puts us out of joint with the universe and so with one another. I think this is what Christ and Buddha knew, the one truth of my existence and yours—the same truth, the same existence, the same Great Heart. Once we even glimpse it, our individual hearts start to pulse with love for all beings, who are beginninglessly inseparable from us. When that pulsing reaches its fullness, we become saints, bodhisattvas, human fountains of healing, dedicated to saving all beings from suffering through the force of our love. And it's nothing dramatic—just a simple, persistent opening to what we are.

Perhaps this silly proverb is really a profound teaching and an urgent invitation from the bodhisattvas to us. They already love us more than we know how to love ourselves; they are directing that force toward us in the silence of this moment, as I write and you read. Had it not been for their love, for its filtering and purifying the negativity with which we pollute the universe, we all might be screaming in some hell realm right now.

But after a certain point we have to get out of the wagon and push. There's a time to be a child of Christ or Mohammed or Ram, and a time to take our place among the grown-ups: they can't clean up after us forever. To reciprocate the love of these eminently lovable saints is the easiest way to start following their example; later we can graduate to loving the other damaged ones like ourselves, the ones who really *need* our love.

In the world to come, we will all be studying with our enemies. They will be our partners . . . After all, as the rabbis say, in empty space there is no right or left.
—RABBI NILTON BONDER

I know two twins who are virtually identical in personality as well as appearance. They're both charming, creative, a little neurotic. But one has things just a bit more together than the other: he's perhaps two or three percent more relaxed, self-confident, conscientious. But that two or three percent has made all the difference. He has a successful marriage, a couple of lovely kids, and a fulfilling career, while his brother, after a string of failed jobs and disastrous relationships, has become a despairing drifter. In the same way, humanity needs to have things just a bit more together to change everything:

The kingdom of heaven is like the yeast a woman took and mixed in with three measures of flour till it was leavened all through.
—MATTHEW 13:33

Just a little more heavenly awareness could leaven our whole society. Our collective consciousness needs to be just two or three percent more luminous, forgiving, loving, and then, as Sam Cooke sang, "What a wonderful world it would be." Perhaps the enlightened ones *have* to be enlightened just to endure the otherwise desolating contrast between the world as it is and the world that so easily could be—it's always just a whisker, just a blip or two of EEG functioning away.

What a wonderful world. The phrase (heard in Sam Cooke's sweet, sad voice) haunts me. My parents raised me to believe it was important to use my life to better the world, to make it a place where peace and justice might prevail. Their vision was to accomplish that through political activism—I grew up marching to ban the bomb, hearing Pete Seeger sing about the workers and the Spanish Civil War, Paul Robeson sing about Joe Hill and John Henry. But I soon suspected that political transformation was not enough. It was literally not radical enough, did not strike close enough to the root of the matter, which is not the system within which we organize ourselves but the compassionate overflow of awareness from within ourselves. Recent history has seen numerous reformers with untransfigured hearts take power, only to rival the horrors perpetrated by the tyrants they overthrew. I never heard my parents speak of Stalin's murders, the rape of Tibet, or the millions who died in the Great Leap Forward. I imagine they were partly blinded by their political idealism, their hope against hope that they had found the doctrine that would transform the world, just as my spiritual idealism has sometimes blinded me.

My parents could never fully endorse the path I chose. They would not understand why I'm on this retreat. They would probably have some caustic comments to make about well-fed Americans sitting on a mountaintop, chanting a meaningless phrase, while the workers carry on the real struggle. (I can hear my father now, in his best Brooklynese, deriding us as a bunch of flakes contemplating their navels.)

But it's not either/or. It *is* important not to use spirituality as a cop-out from social responsibility. The people on this retreat include professors, scientists, therapists, brokers, artists, students, entrepreneurs, *and* political activists, each of whom shines his little light in his own corner as best he can. But they're also devoted to shining a big, shared light from a limitless beacon. We need enlightened, loving politicians, teachers, corporate executives, laborers, professionals . . . and enlightened, loving parents raising enlightened, loving children.

I hope *my* parents, while they were still alive, came to understand (in some quiet corner of their minds or hearts) that with their idealism they made me what I am—that I'm doing what I'm doing to fulfill their vision the best way I know how.

About the Author

Dean Sluyter (rhymes with "lighter") has taught meditation in various parts of the country for more than twenty-five years. An award-winning former film critic, he also teaches English at The Pingry School, where students in his Literature of Enlightenment course explore the nature of awareness through reading, creative writing, and nonsectarian meditative lab work. Dean and his wife, artist–meditation teacher Maggy Sluyter, live in New Jersey.

DATE DUE

MAR 1 4 1998	SEP 0 3 2011
MAY 2 5 1998	
MAY 2 8 1998	
JUN 1 5 1998	
JUN 2 9 1998	
JAN 2 5 2000	
AUG 1 9 2000	
SEP 2 5 2003	
JAN 0 3 2004	
SEP 0 6 2007	
JUN 1 8 2008	